CONFESSIONS OF AN INDIAN IMMIGRANT

Dawn of IT opportunities in the Land of Promise

Aithal

For beloved parents,
Suhas and Anant.

Prologue

Prologue

I came to New York, USA, from Mumbai, India, in 1989. I'm sure every Indian (or any immigrant from other countries) has a story to tell. And their children—born here—roll their eyes, thinking, "here we go again. Yet another snooze-fest." However, I always think of it as an 80-20 rule…80% goes in from one ear and out of the other. However, they absorb 20% of our stories. I, too, am a culprit of repeating my experiences several times (after I crossed fifty, I hope I'm forgiven.) "Dad, I've heard this a million times," our daughter would say as she would look at our son and roll her eyes. They would quickly exchange a 'here-we-go-again' look. However, I know that they would absorb at least 20%.

Things were way different back then. Facebook founder, Mark Zuckerberg, was a 5-year-old. Google founders Larry Page and Sergei Brin were at the ripe age of sixteen. I came to this country when there was no email (technically, it existed but was not widely used. It was mostly used in the universities), no social media, and no smartphones (the current generation has no clue what Thomas Guide[1] is or what a TripTik[2] is.) Pagers were just getting pervasive, and folks were getting used to them. There were phone booths on every street corner. Manhattan's 42nd Street was infested with peep shows. Mugging was rampant. The famous assault now known to us as Central Park 5[3] had occurred just a few days before I arrived in this country and had not completed its 'news cycle' and was still making its rounds in the media. It was a culture shock, coming from a country devoid of gun culture to one that loved guns.

Initially, I thought of making a long, make-your-own title. I would title this book Confessions/Experiences of an Indian Immigrant/Dad (or mom)/husband (or wife). The second

---

[1] Thomas Guide is a series of paperback, spiral-bound atlases featuring detailed street maps of various large metropolitan areas in the United States. Source: Wikipedia.

[2] In the days before Google Maps, Google, or even the internet, a traveler would go to their local AAA branch to plan a road trip. This AAA member would tell the office where they were starting and their intended destination. An agent would draw the route with a highlighter on a series of numbered maps, going through the route with the traveler before they started. The end result, a guided route through a series of maps, was called a TripTik. Source: AAA magazine.

[3] The Central Park jogger case (events also referenced as the Central Park Five Case) was a criminal case in the United States over the aggravated assault and rape of a white woman in Manhattan's Central Park on April 19, 1989, occurring at the same time as an unrelated string of other attacks in the park the same night. Five black and Latino youths were convicted of assaulting the woman, and served sentences ranging from six to twelve years. All later had their charges vacated after a prison inmate confessed to the crime. Source: Wikipedia.

generation (ABCDs[4]) would tend to choose confessions and dad, making it Confessions of an Indian Dad (or mom). In contrast, the first generation parents (FOBs[5]) would prefer experiences and immigrant, creating the title Experiences of an Indian Immigrant/Husband (or wife.) To make the title longer, I thought of having Confessions/Experiences of an/a Indian/(or any other country) Immigrant/Dad(or mom)/ husband(or wife), but it would be an overkill.

Coming from a liberal city like Mumbai (then it was called Bombay) and being a product of intercultural marriage (my dad being a South Indian Brahmin and my mom a Gujarati Jain), I'd pride myself on forward thinking and liberal values. Also, being exposed to two vastly different cultures and traditions made me more aware of typical South Indian and Gujarati thinking. Having a stable (preferably governmental) job would be the ultimate goal of a South Indian household. In contrast, Gujaratis are known to be business-minded. They tend to start their own business (listen to the Patel-Motel Rap[6]). A common joke in India is that a successful business would have a South Indian CEO, but the Chairman would be a Gujarati.

---

[4] **A**merican-**B**orn **C**onfused **D**esi (ABCD) is a term used to refer to South Asian Americans particularly of Indian, Pakistani or Bangladeshi origin, born or raised in the United States, in contrast to those who were born overseas and later settled in the USA. Source: Wikipedia.

[5] **F**resh **O**ff the **B**oat - The term is usually used to describe an immigrant who hasn't yet grasped the customs, language, or culture of the country they're immigrating to. Even if a first-generation of immigrant has assimilated into the American culture and has been living here for decades, he is considered a FOB by the second generation. Source: Google.

[6] https://www.youtube.com/watch?v=cGcENc7J0Oc

The other advantage of coming from a multicultural family is my ability to speak many languages. Not just speak or understand, but to read and write too. Most Indians speak at least two languages. English (a gift from the British) and Hindi (India's official language.) In addition, Mumbai is in the state of Maharashtra—which has Marathi as its state language. On top of these three, I also spoke in my mother tongue (Gujarati—my primary education was in it) and understood a little of my father tongue (Kannada—rhymed with and sometimes misunderstood as Canada).

```
<Begin pet peeve>

Just like Hindi is a language and Hindu is a
religion, Kannada is a language, and Kannadigas
are people from the state of Karnataka who speak
Kannada.

</End pet peeve>
```

These five languages have their own script (well, Hindi and Marathi share a common script.) In addition to these, being a programmer, I also know languages such as Java, C, COBOL, etc. (sorry, lame geek humor.)

Little did I realize how different the value systems are when I compare India and the US. Now, having lived in the country for over three decades, I have evolved (as I have aged), thanks mainly to our daughter (hence, confessions in the title.) Our children look like Indians (brown-skinned,) go to Sunday schools (when they are young), enjoy watching Bollywood movies (with subtitles, of course,) eat Indian food, wear Indian attire, and so on, but they think differently (they are highly independent-minded.) I've noticed that one of the hardest things for the first generation to know is their boundaries. What we take as a concern may be viewed as overbearing by them.

* * *

```
<Begin dad joke>

Q: What's the difference between a FOB and an
ABCD?
A: A FOB is a chikoo, whereas an ABCD is a
coconut?
Q: Why?
A: A chikoo is brown from the inside and outside,
whereas coconut is brown from the outside and
white from the inside.

I warned you it's a dad joke.

</End dad joke>
```

In addition, to a non-Indian, all Indians look the same, but there is a vast difference: in languages, cultural traditions, cuisines, and many more to list here. On many occasions, they may not even speak the same language, thus, defaulting to a common language...you guessed it...English (highly accented with a generous sprinkle of Indian words.)

Most first-generation parents are not good at expressing their feelings (neither am I) in writing. Maybe it's the culture in India or remnants of the Raj-era motto (Keep Calm And Carry On.) However, the second generation is very good at expressing their emotions. So, I request them to pen down the stories we narrate. It would be an invaluable archive for future generations to preserve our memories. Or they will only be alive until the last of the current generation lives.

Personally, I am doing this for my children's benefit. Since childhood, our daughter was always curious to hear my stories. She and our son will be my litmus test. If they find the read engaging, I'll know that I can relate to the next generation. I hope this book sheds some light on a few anecdotes.

This is my attempt to pour down my thoughts as I remember them. I'd love to hear about your experiences. It need not be exclusive to the US. We Indians are spread across the world; thus, I'm very curious to know what the experience of an Indian immigrant is in other parts of the world. Feel free to write to me at author@thegalaxyseries.com.

Also, I would love to hear experiences from folks from other countries. The USA is a land of immigrants. The only people I consider native are the Native Americans. Apart from African Americans (whose ancestors were forcibly brought as enslaved people), we all migrated to this country voluntarily. All of us have a story to tell.

You might be as new as a first or a second-generation American or a fifth or sixth-generation American. If you are not Native American, your ancestors migrated to this country, and I would love to hear about their experiences.

1989-1994

Chapter One

"Do you want coffee?" my wife yelled from the kitchen.

"Of course," I yelled back from my tiny living room. I looked out of the grilled windows from my 1-bedroom ground-floor apartment (flat). Five of us lived there. My parents, my brother, my wife, and I. I grew up in Mumbai's suburb called Vile Parle. Yes, that Vile Parle, where the original factory of the most popular Indian cookies, Parle-G[7], is named after. I lived in a society (apartment complex) called Kripa Nagar since 1969. It consists of a cluster of seven buildings, labeled, A through G. Actually, when my family moved in, there were just two buildings, C and G. It's known as Kripa Nagar to most of its residents, but its formal name is Nutan Jeevan Cooperative Housing Society Ltd.

My wife walked in with a steaming cup of coffee and

---

[7] Parle-G is a brand of biscuits (cookies) manufactured by Parle Products in India. A 2011 Nielsen survey reported that it is the best-selling brand of biscuits in the world. Source: Wikipedia.

placed it on a coaster on the rectangular teapoy in front of me.

"Will you eat *dosa*[8]?" she asked.

I shook my head and continued to browse through the classified section of The Times of India. It was Sunday. Both my parents were home. My father was a manager at a local bank, and my mother was a teacher. She taught English in a vernacular medium[9] (Gujarati) school. In fact, my father was a committee member (treasurer) of our building committee which oversaw construction of other buildings in our society.

My maternal grandfather was a freedom fighter. He would narrate his experiences before India got its independence in 1947. He always used to wear clothes made out of khadi[10]. As I write this sentence, I just realized that all the parents of my generation were born

---

[8] A dosa is a thin batter-based dish (usually crispy) originating from South India, made from a fermented batter predominantly consisting of lentils and rice. Its main ingredients are rice and black gram, ground together in a fine, smooth batter with a dash of salt, then fermented. Dosas are a common dish in South Indian cuisine, but now have been popular all over the Indian subcontinent. Dosas are served hot along with chutney by tradition and sambar in recent times. Chutney is a fine paste made up of groundnut, coconut and lentil. Source: Wikipedia.

[9] Vernacular medium schools are schools where the medium of education is a local or native language. Source: Wikipedia.

[10] Khadi is a hand-spun and woven natural fiber cloth promoted by Mahatma Gandhi as swadeshi (self-sufficiency) for the freedom struggle of the Indian subcontinent, Source: Wikipedia.

under British rule. My grandmother was a soft-spoken, sweet lady. At the risk of creating controversy among my maternal cousins, I maintain that I was her favorite.

```
<Begin confession>

Being the firstborn from both—my father's and my
mother's—sides, I was pampered a lot.

</End confession>
```

My wife had recently become a teacher at her alma mater. She was teaching arts at her college. She was helping my mother in the kitchen while my father sat near the window, watching passers-by. My mother had sent my younger brother to run some errands.

I reached for the cup and blew gently on the surface before taking a sip while my eyes continued to scan lazily down the classifieds. I wasn't too sure what I was looking for. A new employment? Maybe.

I was working for a small software development company as a programmer. I felt that my career had stagnated. I was newly married. I had more responsibilities now. I was ready for a jump. Looking back, I think I was curious to see what kind of opportunities were out there. Going to the US was nowhere on my radar. Plus, I didn't have a degree in engineering or computer science. I had done my B.Sc. in Physics at Mithibai College—a local college- and obtained a degree from the University of Mumbai. Mithibai, well, it was formally called Mithibai College of Arts, Chauhan

Institute of Science & Amruthben Jivanlal College of Commerce and Economics. No one called it that, referring to it merely as Mithibai (or 'Sweet Lady'—a lame joke.) The word Mithibai is actually two words combined together, Mithi (sweet) and bai (lady) thus making it Sweet Lady (I told you it's lame.)

Suddenly, my eyes narrowed as they fell upon a small squared column that advertised a course on mainframe computers. *Mainframes?* I thought. I had never worked on them. I was a PC guy programming in COBOL[11]. My curiosity rose. I focused on it and started to read.

```
Learn to program on an IBM mainframe with CICS[12].
If selected, you will get a chance to travel to
the US for an assignment.
- Mafatlal Consultancy, Worli, Bombay.
```

Did I tell you Mumbai was called Bombay then? It was a name more convenient to pronounce (and remember) by the British when they ruled India. A few decades after they left, the original names were restored. Bombay became Mumbai, Madras became Chennai, Trichy became Tiruchirappalli, Cochin became Kochi, Vizag became Visakhapatnam, and so on. There are too many names to

---

[11] COBOL (an acronym for "common business-oriented language") is a compiled English-like computer programming language designed for business use. Source: Wikipedia.

[12] CICS stands for Customer Information Control System. It is a general-purpose transaction processing subsystem for the z/OS operating system. Source: IBM.

list.

But I digress. I was excited—not at the prospect of going to the US. I could finally get my hands on a mainframe. Although PCs were pervasive and small-sized businesses could afford them, mainframes were not. Only large corporations and IT companies had them. In addition to the cost, there also is a question of space. They are large and bulky and require a temperature-controlled and dust-free room. Only a few people were allowed to go into the enclosed room.

I have worked on various operating systems, including Unix, MS-DOS (predecessor of Windows), and CP/M[13] (oh boy, I feel like I'm listing my skills in a resume.)

<Begin geek trivia>

---

[13] CP/M, originally standing for Control Program/Monitor and later Control Program for Microcomputers, is an operating system created for a mass-market in 1974 for Intel 8080/85-based microcomputers

```
As a newbie programmer, I didn't know the
difference between MS-DOS and CP/M. Both of them
had a DIR command to list the files. However, I
would press Ctrl-C to stop the listing. Little
did I know that Ctrl-C was the key combination to
reboot the PC on CP/M. I still remember the
amused look on my colleague sitting next to me
when he saw my baffled expression, as he tried
very hard not to burst out laughing.

</End geek trivia>
```

This was an excellent opportunity to list the mainframe as a skill that would allow me to apply for better paying jobs.

This is it, I thought. I decided to take the course.

"*Pappaji*," I said aloud.

"Yes?" my father replied without turning his head. He continued to peer at the passers-by.

"This looks interesting," I said as I got up and walked across where he was sitting. I tapped with my index finger on the square box on the paper.

"What do you think?" He turned his head and looked at the newspaper. "Hmm." He grunted as he scanned the classifieds. "Do you want to do it?" he looked at me over the rims of his glasses.

"Yes."

"Why? Do you want to go to the US?"

"That's not why," I shook my head. "I want to learn CICS to further my career. Besides, it clearly says, 'if selected.' There will be many candidates that might be more qualified than me, more experienced folks with a master's or an engineering degree and probably having worked on mainframes (I only was in the field for three years, and that too, my experience was exclusively confined to PCs). A B.Sc. graduate from a college popular for its 'filmy' crowd won't stand a chance."

"Filmy," he smiled. Mithibai was known as a filmy college as many film stars sent their children there. It boasts vast alumni and alumnae of actors, directors, musicians, etc., who have graduated from Mithibai.

One such alumna that comes to my mind is Nita Ambani. She is the owner of a highly successful cricket franchise, my beloved Mumbai Indians.

```
<Begin confession>

Like most Indians, I, too, am a huge cricket fan.
And like them, it's in my DNA.

</End confession>

<Begin shameless plug>

In my first book, India Was One (available on
Amazon in paperback and Kindle format, both in
the US and India), I have dedicated an entire
chapter to cricket.

</End shameless plug>

<Begin cricket trivia>

Mumbai Indians' home ground is the Wankhede
Stadium in South Mumbai. I was at the stadium for
its inaugural match held between India and the
mighty West Indies in January of 1975. I still
remember the West Indies captain, Clive Lloyd,
scoring a swashbuckling 242. To put things in
perspective, the most famous cricketer in the
world—Sachin Tendulkar—was two-year-old at the
```

time.

```
</End cricket trivia>
```

She, Nita Ambani, also happens to be the wife of one of the wealthiest men in Asia, Mukesh Ambani, with a net worth of 87.5 billion USD[14]. He also happens to be of the top-fifteen wealthiest people in the world—enough about money. Coming back to Nita Ambani, I've seen her in the Canteen, a cafeteria sandwiched between two colleges, Mithibai and NM.

```
<Begin shameless plug>

I have a chapter titled The Canteen in my first
book, India Was One  (available on Amazon in
paperback and Kindle format, both in the US and
India)

</End shameless plug>
```

When I was younger, we used to have a cricket match every Sunday between Seniors and Juniors. I was the captain of Seniors.

```
<Begin confession>

We, the Seniors, never won a single match. Yes,
```

---

[14] Mukesh Dhirubhai Ambani is an Indian business magnate, chairman, managing director, and the largest shareholder of Reliance Industries Ltd. (RIL), a Fortune Global 500 company and India's most valuable company by market value. According to Forbes and Bloomberg Billionaires Index, Ambani's net worth is estimated at US$86.3 billion as of 4 July 2022

```
I'm embarrassed to admit my failure as a captain
now (after decades). I'm sure that a Junior (my
brother was in the Juniors) will be reading this
gleefully.

</End confession>
```

Each side could play for one-hundred-twenty balls, and the opposing team would chase the target within the ball limit. This was in the 70s. So, yes, you guessed it.

```
<Begin controversial statement>

We started the T20 cricket.

</End controversial statement>
```

Although, we didn't call it that. Do I know if it's true? Of course not. But as Bill Maher[15] says, I just 'feel' it's true.

"I think you should do it," said a voice behind me. I turned around. My mother was standing in the door frame that led into the hallway.

"I agree," my wife shouted from the kitchen.

"Do you even know what it is?" I yelled back as I laughed.

"No, but I'm sure it must be something important to you. I've never seen you going through the classifieds."

"She has a point," my mother nodded.

"Okay," my father said as he handed me the newspaper.

---

[15] William Maher is an American comedian, actor, political commentator, and television host. Source: Wikipedia.

"Great," I beamed, "I'll enroll tomorrow."

*_*_*

I dialed Mafatlal's number on my recently acquired rotary phone the following day. *What's a rotary phone,* you ask? The ancestors of smartphones.

Back then, phones were not ubiquitous. One had to apply for a landline to the government and wait. It took years (yes, years and not days or months) to get a phone connection. My father had applied for one years ago, and our turn had finally come. In fact, many households covered the phone with a blusher (as if it was a freshly wedded bride). Two instruments folks covered with blushers were their phones and televisions (started in Mumbai in 1972—twenty-five years after India's independence from the British—that too, in black and white, very few channels and for only a few hours in the evening.) People (mainly mom-n-pop businesses) would have a lock on their phones to prohibit unwanted outgoing calls (butt-dialing). Only incoming calls were allowed. Why? Because they were free.

* * *

Once again, I digress.

After a few rings, a melodious voice answered. "Mafatlal Consulting. How may I help you?"

"Hello," I said, "I saw the ad for the CICS course in the Times of India."

"Yes?"

"I am interested in enrolling in it."

"Great," her voice perked up.

"But before I do so, I have a few questions."

"Sure," she continued in her sing-song voice.

"How long is the course? It doesn't mention the duration."

"Oh, I'm sorry," she apologized, but her voice sounded facetious. "Six weeks."

"And will I get hands-on training?"

"What do you mean?" she sounded confused.

"Will I be working on a terminal, or will they be all whiteboard theories?"

"Ah, you mean practicals?" she exclaimed.

"Yes."

"Of course."

"Great," I said as a smile spread across my face. I was finally going to get my hands on a mainframe. "I'd like to enroll in it." She wrote down my name to reserve a spot. I informed her that I'd be coming in the afternoon to pay the fees (cash, of course. We didn't have credit cards back in those days, or at least, *I* didn't have one. Remember, I come from a middle-class family and a culture where cash was king.)

The course was commencing a few months later. However, she had informed me that there were limited spots, and she had received many people inquiring about the course. I was alarmed that so many people had shown interest in enrolling in it in less than twenty-four hours after the classified ad came out. I decided to go in the morning. I called my office and informed them I'd not be coming in. I quickly showered, got dressed, and stepped out in the sweltering heat. I looked at the clear sky, devoid of clouds. *I hope it doesn't rain today,* I thought. Unlike most Mumbaikars, I never carried an umbrella (I wanted to look cool.)

Worli (where Mafatlal's office is located) is about forty-five minutes by bus ride from Irla, Vile Parle (where I lived). I walked to the bus stop and got onto a red-colored BEST[16] displaying 84Exp. as its route number. I got off at Worli. I crossed the road and entered Mafatlal

---

[16] The Brihanmumbai Electricity Supply and Transport (BEST) is a civic transport and electricity provider public body based in Mumbai, Maharashtra, India.

Consultancy's office, relieved to be in an air-conditioned environment, away from the muggy climate outside. A young receptionist was sitting behind a desk, attending to the phone. She wore a navy blue saree and a red blouse. I approached her. "I'll be with you," she mouthed as she continued to nod. After a minute or so, she hung up and looked at me. "Yes?" she smiled.

"I'm here for the CICS course. I called earlier. Did I speak with you?"

"Yes," she smiled as she looked down at her notepad where she had scribbled my name. "Is this you?" she asked as she placed it between us. "Yes," I nodded.

"Great," she smiled as she opened a drawer, produced a form, and handed it to me. "Please fill in your details."

I filled in the form, handed it to her, and reached into my pocket. She took it, briefly scanned it, and extended her other hand. I gave her the cash (Rs.5,000, if I remember correctly. The exchange rate was 1 US dollar to 13.92 Indian Rupee. It's ballooned to around 79 Indian Rupee now.)

"Thank you," she said as she counted the bills. She nodded with a smile as she counted the last bill. She placed my form in a pile in a tray marked, 'enrollees.' I wondered how many had already enrolled in the course. "How many have you accepted so far?" I asked.

"About fifteen."

Fifteen?! Already?! I started to feel fortunate that I'd enrolled early. "Wow!" I exclaimed. "That was fast."

"Yes," she smiled, "good that you called in and enrolled

so early. It's on a first-come-first-serve basis. We have been getting many inquiries. I'm sure the course will be full by the end of the day."

"How many do you enroll?"

"We top off at fifty."

"Oh," I felt lucky that I was in. "Is there any course material for me to study?"

"No," she shook her head. "Just bring a notepad."

"Okay," I smiled. "Thank you."

"You are welcome."

I was eager to inform my family of the good news, but I had to wait until I got home (remember, no mobile phones?) I stepped out in the heat and looked around. There was a small *paan*[17] shop. I was not a big *paan* person, but I knew that it also sold cigarettes (yes, like most Indian youngsters who wanted to look cool and impress girls, I used to smoke back then. A nasty habit that I've given up for over twenty years. My wife hated it and was overjoyed when I gave it up.)

I waited for the 84Exp. at the bus stop that would take me back. Upon returning home, I informed my wife (the only one at home, the rest had gone to work.) I was in time for lunch, but I celebrated it with a chilled beer. Although it wasn't much of an achievement, I felt this would lead somewhere.

---

[17] Betel nut chewing, also called betel quid chewing or areca nut chewing, is a practice in which areca nuts are chewed together with slaked lime and betel leaves for their stimulant and narcotic effects.

* * *

Chapter Two

After enrolling in the course, I went back to my regular life. I was doing a 9-to-5 job and spending time with my family and friends in the evening. I had many friends: childhood friends, school friends, college friends, society (the place where I lived since 1969) friends, karate friends (yes, I was a karate student), and friends that didn't fit into these categories.

Once, my wife and I decided to go out for a romantic dinner. Since the restaurant was nearby, we decided to walk—a bad idea. I bumped into a friend of mine who talked for a long time. My wife patiently waited for the conversation to get over so we could be alone again. However, to her disappointment, my friend invited himself to dinner.

And to make matters worse, the restaurant owner was my friend. So, he too decided to join us. And because of that, six servers were attending to our needs, hovering over us, making my wife highly uncomfortable as she ate. Needless to say, she was furious. I avoided meeting her eyes, fearing that her daggered, angry looks would kill me. So much for a romantic dinner.

Once again, I digress (it probably is a highly annoying pattern by now. However, in my defense, this is my style of narrating a story. So please bear with me.) Soon it was time for my course to start. It was conducted in the evening (6 PM to 9 PM) to make it convenient for working folks. I left my workplace, which was in South Bombay (aka Town), and caught a bus to Worli. I was excited and nervous at the same time. Excited that I was finally going to learn CICS and nervous that I'd be the least educated in the class.

I entered Mafatlal's office and saw the familiar face of the receptionist. She was getting ready to leave for the day.

"Hi," I said nervously.

She looked up, and a smile spread across her face as she recognized me.

"Oh, hello." She had a very melodious voice.

"Hi," I repeated more confidently this time. "Where is the course being conducted?"

"Upstairs," she pointed at the flight of stairs. "Room 103 on the first floor."

"Thank you," I nodded as I walked toward the stairs.

```
<Begin trivia>

You must be wondering why the first floor is
upstairs. Aren't you already on the first floor?
Not in India. The floors begin with the ground
floor, the first floor, the second floor, and so
```

on. It's one of the terminologies Americans have difficulty wrapping their heads around. Remember, we were ruled by the British for hundreds of years. Hence, we have adopted certain words in our language that would be a no-no in America. For example, a fag to denote a cigarette, a rubber to denote an eraser, and so on. There are innumerable words. Also, India spells English as the British do. Colour instead of color, tyre instead of tire, etc. In addition, Indians have their own hybrid language known as Hinglish (you guessed it, a combination of Hindi and English.) It has two main variations. One: A sentence that is in Hindi but is peppered with English words (that's a little easier to understand), and two: a word that is a made-up one with a mixture of Hindi and English. These words are more regional and colloquial. For example, take the word 'muskafy.' A person from Mumbai would know what it means; however, a person from, say, New Delhi wouldn't. BTW, muskafy is a combination of muska (butter) and fy, with muska being a very Mumbai word. So when someone says, 'stop mauskafying me,' s/he is saying, 'stop brown-nosing me.'

</End trivia>

I found room 103. With apprehension, I entered. It was a rectangular room with a large whiteboard at the far end. A bank of tables with a narrow aisle running through it in the middle from the door I had entered to the whiteboard. Three people occupied each set of tables. There were ten rows. I mentally started counting. "10 rows and 2 columns. Each column occupies 3 students. So, 6 per row." The receptionist was right. They had capped it at fifty. Yes, there were fifty of us.

I scanned the room. A man turned around and smiled.

I smiled back as I instantly recognized him. "Rajul!" I exclaimed. "Hi!" A sense of relief spread through me. "Come here," he beckoned. The seat next to him was unoccupied. He gestured at it with his eyes. *Sit next to me,* he was saying. I smiled and walked to the seat. He patted the empty bench as he slid back to make a place for me. I slid into the seat, looked at him, and smiled. "Hi," I shook his hand. "So good to see you." There were many empty tables, but in a few minutes, most of them were occupied as students started to pour in. I was scanning their faces, looking for a familiar one, but alas, I didn't recognize any other. I turned to him. "What have you been doing?"

"Same as you," he smiled, "programming."

I was about to say something when a voice said aloud, "Excuse me." I turned and looked up. A spectacled man was standing, looking unsure. "Is this seat taken?" I shook my head. He smiled, slid into it, and proffered his hand. "Hi, I'm Rahul." I shook his hand, introducing myself. Rajul, too, did the same, both leaning across my tilted torso.

A word about Rajul. Although he is from a different college, he used to frequent the Canteen (yes, THAT Canteen. Should I shamelessly plug my first book again to jog your memory?) After I graduated, I was in search of a job. My father was working at a bank in a place called Dongri. It is about an hour's train ride from my residence. I was supposed to meet him at his office. After catching a train from Andheri Station, I changed to the Harbour

Line[18] at Bandra Railway Station to Reach my final destination, Masjid. I stepped out of the shaded station to the beating sun. I was already sweating. I hurried to the bank to meet my father, weaving through the hawkers, carts loaded with oversized cotton bales, and crowds of people going about their business. Suddenly, a voice shouted across the narrow street. "Hey, buddy." I turned to look in that direction. I wasn't sure if it was calling me until my eyes fell upon a familiar face. "Rajul," I smiled as I crossed the street and shook his hand. "What are you doing here?" he asked. I told him that I was meeting my father. "How about you? What are you doing here?" I asked.

"A part-time job," he said.

"Part-time?" I raised my eyebrows.

"Yeah, man," he smiled sheepishly as he proceeded to tell me that the job was only for a few hours a week. "How about you? Are you doing anything?"

"Not yet," I shook my head. I informed him about my interest in computers. He smiled. "Want a job?"

"Of course," I eagerly replied.

"Come, follow me." He started to walk.

"What? Now?"

"Yes...unless you are getting late to meet your father."

"No," I quickly shook my head, "I have some time."

---

[18] The Harbour line is a branch line of the Mumbai Suburban Railway operated by Central Railway. It was named so because it catered to the eastern neighborhoods along the city's natural harbor. Source: Wikipedia.

"Okay, then," he said as he started walking, and I followed him. He led me to what looked like a shop with a godown(warehouse). There is no equivalent of it in the US. The closest comparison can be a loading dock of a distribution center. Piles of oversized bales were stacked to the ceiling. A man was sleeping on one of them. He woke up when he saw Rajul.

"*Kem cho* (how are you), Rajulbhai?" he greeted.

"*Majhama* (I'm well. Actually, the literal translation is joyous, however, it's a standard reply by Gujarati folks)," he replied. "*Seth che?* (Is the boss in?)"

"*Na*," the man shook his head.

I was curious now. I looked around. "What is this place?"

"Oh, right," he looked at me and smiled. "It's a transport company. I work here part-time as a data entry operator. The work is sporadic. When a truck comes in, I have to enter the challans[19] of its cargo. We have a small cabin upstairs that houses the computer. It's already loaded with an accounting package. The work is not demanding." He raised his eyebrows. "So?"

"So, what?" I was confused.

"Are you interested?"

---

[19] Challan or Chalan is a common Hindi word that has become an Indian English technical word used officially in many professional, especially financial transactions. It usually means an official form or receipt of acknowledgement or other kind of proof document, piece of paperwork, police citation, etc. Source: Wikipedia.

I was taken aback by this unexpected turn of events. When I left my house in the morning, little did I imagine I'd be offered a job—and that too without an interview. I didn't know what to say. Rajul sensed my hesitation. "Can I call you tonight?"

That will give me time to talk with my family, I thought.

"Sure," he nodded.

"Thanks, *yaar* (buddy)."

"You are most welcome. Good, I'll talk to the owner. Don't worry. It's just a formality. Consider you have the job." And then he said the thing that was on top of my mind. "You'll get Rs.500 per month." In case you are an Indian and mentally converting into dollars, allow me to help you. At the time of writing this book, the exchange rate is 79.48. So yes, my first salary in the field of computers was whopping…drumroll, please…$6.29 per month.

--*

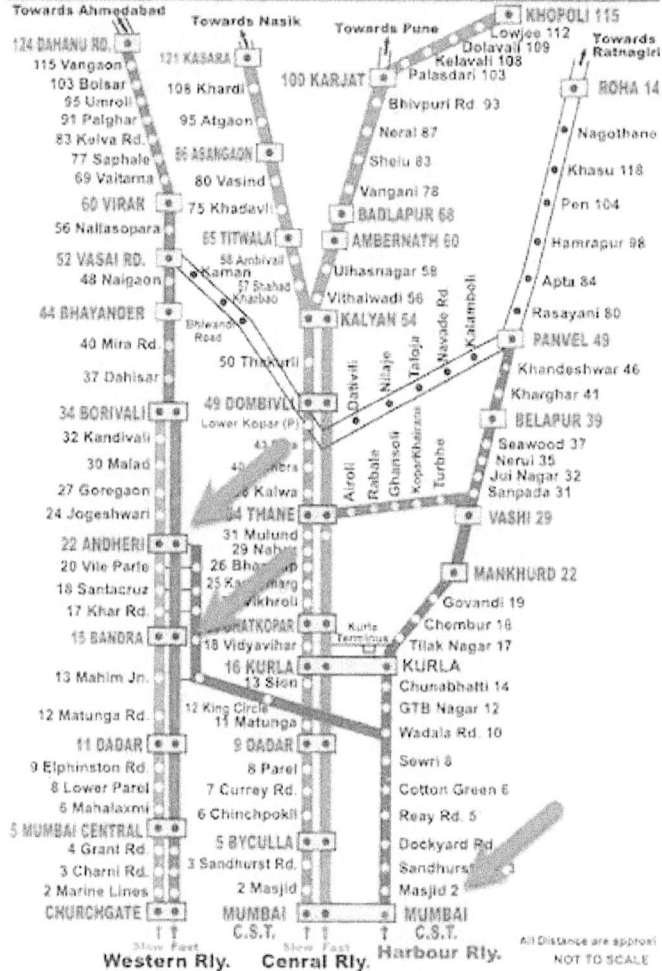

WESTERN, CENTRAL, HARBOUR LOCAL RAIL NETWORK

Towards Ahmedabad
Towards Nasik
Towards Pune
● KHOPOLI 115
Lowjee 112
Dolavali 109
Towards Ratnagiri
Kelavali 108
Palasdari 103
124 DAHANU RD.
121 KASARA
100 KARJAT
ROHA 14
115 Vangaon
108 Khardi
Bhivpuri Rd 93
103 Bolsar
95 Umroli
95 Atgaon
Neral 87
Nagothane
91 Palghar
83 Kolva Rd.
86 ASANGAON
Shelu 83
Khasu 118
77 Saphale
80 Vasind
Vangani 78
Pen 104
69 Vaitarna
60 VIRAR
75 Khadavli
BADLAPUR 68
Hamragur 98
56 Nallasopara
65 TITWALA
AMBERNATH 60
52 VASAI RD.
58 Ambivali
Saman
Ulhasnagar 58
Apta 84
48 Naigaon
57 Shahad
Vithalwadi 56
Rasayani 80
44 BHAYANDER
Khabao
Bhiwandi
KALYAN 54
PANVEL 49
40 Mira Rd.
Road
50 Thakurli
Khandeshwar 46
37 Dahisar
Kharghar 41
34 BORIVALI
49 DOMBIVLI
BELAPUR 39
32 Kandivali
Lower Kopar (P)
Seawood 37
30 Malad
Mumbra
Nerul 35
27 Goregaon
Kalwa
Jui Nagar 32
24 Jogeshwari
34 THANE
Sanpada 31
22 ANDHERI
31 Mulund
VASHI 29
20 Vile Parle
29 Nahur
26 Bhandup
MANKHURD 22
18 Santacruz
25 Kanjur Marg
Govandi 19
17 Khar Rd.
Vikhroli
Chembur 18
15 BANDRA
GHATKOPAR
Kurla
Tilak Nagar 17
18 Vidyavihar
Terminus
13 Mahim Jn.
16 KURLA
KURLA
13 Sion
Chunabhatti 14
12 Matunga Rd.
12 King Circle
GTB Nagar 12
11 Matunga
Wadala Rd. 10
11 DADAR
9 DADAR
Sewri 8
9 Elphinston Rd.
8 Parel
Cotton Green 6
8 Lower Parel
7 Currey Rd.
Reay Rd. 5
6 Mahalaxmi
6 Chinchpokli
Dockyard Rd.
5 MUMBAI CENTRAL
5 BYCULLA
Sandhurst
4 Grant Rd.
3 Sandhurst Rd.
Masjid 2
3 Charni Rd.
2 Masjid
2 Marine Lines
CHURCHGATE
MUMBAI
MUMBAI
C.S.T.
C.S.T.
All Distances are approx
Slow Fast
Slow Fast
NOT TO SCALE
Western Rly.   Cenral Rly.   Harbour Rly.

As the course progressed, Rajul, Rahul, and I naturally

30

gravitated toward each other. It may have to do with the age thing. We were around the same age and had a similar sense of humor. We would always sit together at the same table. If one were running late, we would save a spot for him.

Towards the end of the course, we (all of us, the entire class) were informed that we would be meeting a businessman from America. If selected, we would be traveling to New York for an assignment. He would be interviewing us in the last week of the course. We were all excited. I allowed myself to dream about going to America.

In the last week of the class, our instructor told us that the man had arrived in India and would be coming to the office. That evening, I was a nervous wreck. I started to question my lack of command of English. Coming from a vernacular medium, English was not a second (ESL-English as a Second Language, as the teachers here call it) language but a third language (ETL?). The first was Gujarati, the second being the national language, Hindi, and then English. Fortunately, my English was better than most of my schoolmates because of my father. He had insisted on talking to me in English when I was in the sixth grade. *Thank you, Pappaji.*

```
<Begin tangent>

My wife (who is from an English medium school)
would make fun of me when I told her that our
essay was prewritten with a few words left blank.
We were only required to fill in the blanks.
```

</End tangent>

The following day, I got up early. As I was getting dressed, my mother shoved a spoonful of sweet yogurt in my mouth.

"What is it?" I was annoyed.

"For good luck," she replied.

"C'mon, *mummy*, I'm not going for a test."

"It doesn't matter." Over the years, I had learned not to argue with her. I had mentally compromised that I'd silently let her do these rituals, even if I disagreed. As long as it didn't inconvenience me and made her happy, it was fine. Growing up in a culture where ancient rituals surround you, one tends to accept them for 'peace of mind.'

"So, is it a Hindu thing or a Jain thing?" I gave a sarcastic smile. "Or should I ask, A South Indian or a North Indian custom?"

"*Chup* (quiet)," she glared at me.

"Yes, *mummy*, what is it?" my brother smirked. Shaking her head in anger, she stormed out of the room. Continuing to get dressed, I tucked my shirt in and lifted the collar to wear a tie.

<Begin confession>

I had never worn a tie in my life before that.

</End Confession>

My brother smiled when he saw the expression on my

face. "Do you know how to?"

"Of course." I lied confidently. Being the elder brother, I didn't want to expose myself. He sensed my lies. "Here, let me help you." He came over, flung a tie around my neck, and skillfully tied a knot. "Where did you learn?" I was impressed. "Our neighbor taught me," he beamed proudly.

I thanked him and quickly stepped out of my house, praying my friends would't see me in this attire. They were sure to make fun of me. Thankfully, I didn't bump into any of them and headed for the bus stop to catch 84Exp.

Chapter Three

When I reached Mafatlal, the receptionist directed me to a conference room.

"They are waiting for you," she smiled, "good luck." She went back to the letter she was formatting on her typewriter.

"Thank you," I mumbled as I started to walk towards the hallway that led inside. *They? As in more than one?* I panicked. *I thought that there would be only one.* As I approached the conference room, I saw Rahul exiting it with a big smile. "Hey, buddy." I wanted to say hey back, but my throat was dry. "H—hey," I croaked. "How did it go?

"It went well."

"Did you get it?"

"I think so; I'll know in the evening."

"I thought the instructor told us there would be only a single man."

"That's right."

"But the receptionist told me, 'they are waiting.' So, is

there more than one inside?"

"Yes," he nodded, "but there's only one from America. The other two are Mafatlal employees. They are there to ensure that the interview runs smoothly." He then winked and grinned, "I think they are there to interpret our heavy accent…just in case."

"Oh, I see," I nodded, trying to hide my nervousness. "Did he have any trouble understanding you?"

"No," he shook his head. "Just make sure you speak slowly, clearly, and enunciate every word." I nervously adjusted my tie. He must have sensed my apprehension. "Don't worry; you'll be fine." He gently patted me on my back to reassure me. "Good luck." He started walking towards the reception area. I could hear him whistling softly, but it sounded loud as it echoed through the corridor. I envied the position he was in. He must have entered feeling nervous, not knowing the outcome, and successfully coming out at the other end.

I psyched myself to look at the positives. My interview was in the morning; hence, the interviewer would be fresh (less tired.) Just like me, Rahul and Rajul had bachelor's degrees. They, too, were not engineers. My instructor had told me that I was in the top 10% of the class. (So, that was encouraging. In other words, I was not dumb.) I did a mental-math. Let's say I'm in the top 10%. So, five students (there were fifty of us.) Out of which Rahul has already done well. So, let's assume that he gets selected. That would leave four spots empty. Suddenly, my chances started looking good. A faint smile spread across my face.

My confidence improved. I began to feel better. My gait changed.

The glass doors to the conference room were shut. It was enclosed in glass walls that were translucent five feet up from the floor for privacy and then transparent to the ceiling. I could make out three shapes. The only thing that was clearly visible was the top of their heads. Two sets of black hair and one set of almost white. *This must be the businessman,* I thought. I adjusted my tie, changed my facial expression to a broad smile, and pushed open the door.

*_*_*

Donn Liles is one of the pioneers of the ubiquity of Indian IT professionals. He first came to India in 1978, before Windows[20] or the MAC OS[21] was released, and I still was a high school student. To put things in perspective, Star Wars was released a year before. Indian superstar, Amitabh Bachchan, had three biggest hits of his career: Don, Trishul, and Muqaddar Ka Sikandar (and, by the way, he still is one of the leading superstars in Bollywood. Boy, talk about staying power!)

---

[20] Windows 1.0 is the first major release of Microsoft Windows, a family of graphical operating systems for personal computers developed by Microsoft. It was first released to manufacturing in the United States on November 20, 1985. Source: Wikipedia.

[21] The Macintosh "System 1" is the first version of Apple Macintosh operating system and the beginning of the classic Mac OS series. System 1 was released on January 24, 1984. Source: Wikipedia.

He, Donn, owned a company called Data Basics Corp. (DBC) in New York. His company had developed a package called CAMP (Comprehensive Apparel Manufacturers' Package) for the US textile and apparel industry. It was a piece of software created for IBM Mainframes and then ported to AS/400[22] (their predecessor being System/36[23] and System/38[24]). All of these were monstrous in their size compared to the current computers. The sheer dimensions of them required a big area.

---

[22] The IBM AS/400 (Application System/400) is a family of midrange computers from IBM announced in June 1988 and released in August 1988. It was the successor to the System/36 and System/38 platforms, and ran the OS/400 operating system. Lower-cost but more powerful than its predecessors, the AS/400 was extremely successful at launch, with an estimated 111,000 installed by the end of 1990. Source: Wikipedia.

[23] The IBM System/36 (often abbreviated as S/36) was a midrange computer marketed by IBM - a multi-user, multi-tasking successor to the System/34. Source: Wikipedia.

[24] The System/38 is a discontinued minicomputer and midrange computer manufactured and sold by IBM.

IBM System/36

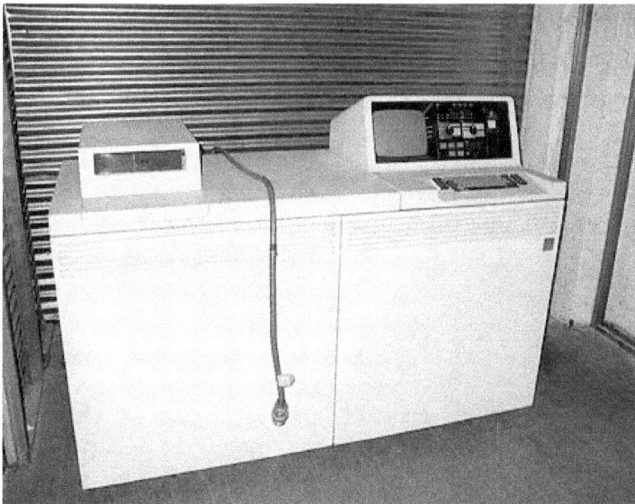

IBM System/38

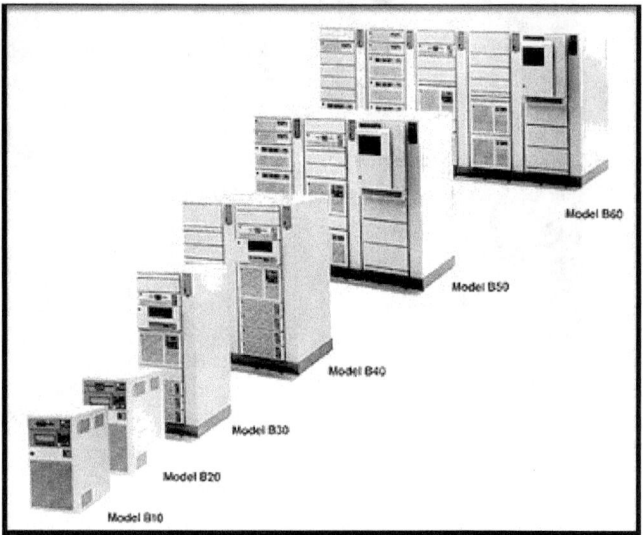

IBM AS/400 Family in 1988

They only had green-screen, text-based terminals, no
GUI (Graphical User Interface); hence no mouse, so no
point-n-click capability. The largest configured S/36
could support 7MB of RAM and 1478MB of disk space.
This cost over US$200,000 back in the early 1980s
(compare these specs with the smartphone in your back
pocket and laugh.)

<Begin note>

A note about AS/400. Although it lacks fancy
graphics, it's a workhorse. The current model is
still very much in the industry. One of the most
visible uses of it I've witnessed is when I go to
Costco. I see the familiar green screen terminals
at their helpdesk. They use it to look up an

item.

</End note>

Coming back to Donn Liles, he's definitely instrumental in making the Indian IT industry known worldwide. He had started hiring consultants from India in the late 70s. Words such as outsourcing, BPO, and many other such acronyms didn't even exist then.

--*

There was an oval-shaped table in the center of the room surrounded by a dozen chairs. A tray with a jug of water and four empty glasses lay on it. The floor was covered with a blue rug. There was a small credenza on one side. Since the room had glass walls, it was devoid of any decorative hangings. On one side, on the far end of the table, stood a whiteboard with Welcome scribbled in blue marker.

Three men were standing near the table, two Indians and one American. Both the Indians sported a mustache, one very thick and one thin. All of them wore suits; however, it was obvious that the two Indians were not used to wearing one. On the other hand, it hung on the American like a second skin.

One of the Indians, Mr.V. (let's call him that for privacy,) smiled. "Hello," he nodded as he ceremoniously waved his hand toward the American, "This is Mr….,"

But before he finished his sentence, the American smiled widely and proffered his hand, "Hi, I'm Donn

Liles." I shook his hand (confidently but not vigorously. I hope it wasn't sweaty.)

"Hello, Mr. Donn Liles," I blurted out his full name. I know, I know, I'm not supposed to do that. But hey, I was nervous. He must have sensed it. He smiled, "call me Donn."

"Hello, Mr. Donn."

"No," he laughed, "just Donn."

"Hello, Donn," I felt awkward. In our culture, we never address anyone by their first name if they are older than us. Even if they are as old as us but don't know them, we address them by their last name.

Donn was a spectacled man with curly white hair. His eyes twinkled when he smiled. He wore a gray suit and a red tie. He wore freshly polished black shoes. He sat down in one of the chairs and motioned at me to do the same. The two Indians sat across the table and casually leaned in.

"So, tell me about yourself." Faint lines formed at the corner of his deep blue eyes as he smiled. Suddenly, I was aware that the three men intently listened to what came out of my mouth next. They were not concerned about my skills or qualifications but paid attention to how I spoke. It was essential that I communicated well.

`<Begin confession>`

`I had never spoken with a non-Indian before this.`
`Here I am, up close and personal, shaking hands`
`of a white man (with deep blue eyes that I had`
`only seen in Hollywood movies.)`

* * *

```
</End confession>
```

"Well," I started, making sure I was speaking clearly and deliberately. It felt more like an audition than an interview. If the world is a stage, a job interview indeed is an audition, isn't it? As I progressed, I felt more confident when I saw Donn nodding. It told me that he understood what I was saying. I don't remember how long it was, but it felt like an eternity. When I was done, Donn smiled. "Excellent." He looked at Mr.V.'s colleague, Mr.J. (name withheld for privacy), and gave a faint nod. It was hardly discernible, but my hyper-senses picked it up. I knew that I was selected.

I didn't want to blow my chances by saying anything stupid. I got up from my chair. They all did the same. I shook Donn's hand. "Thank you; it was a pleasure meeting you."

"Thank you; the pleasure was entirely mine. Have a wonderful day."

```
<Begin confession>

I'm grateful to him for giving me the opportunity
to come to the US. I wish someone would make a
documentary on his journey. ** Hint, hint Ken
Burns25 **

</End confession>
```

---

[25] Kenneth Lauren Burns is an American filmmaker, known for his style of using archival footage and photographs in documentary films. Source: Wikipedia.

* * *

*_*_*

Feeling like a million dollars, I sauntered out of the conference room. I did well in the interview. I remembered the little nod of approval and felt more confident (I felt as if I had grown a few inches taller—maybe because I was walking on a cloud.)

As I was heading towards the reception area, Mr. V. came out and stopped me. "Hey."

I turned around. "Yes?"

I could tell from his smile that I had fared well in the interview.

"Congratulations."

I was pleasantly surprised at the rapid turn of events.

"For what?" Although I knew what he was alluding to, I didn't want to jump to any conclusions.

"You are in; he wants you."

I was stunned. I didn't know how to react. I wanted to run and hug him, but my professional instincts stopped me from doing anything stupid. Besides, Indian men are not supposed to hug or show overt emotions (remember the British motto—Keep Calm and Carry On.)

"That's great news," I replied, acting cool on the outside, but my heart was jumping with joy inside. "When do I go?"

"Well," he said, "first, there are a few things that need to be taken care of."

"Such as?"

"You'll need to tender your resignation from your current job and work for us."

That's not a big thing, I thought. *I can do it today. I don't even have to give them two weeks' notice. I'm sure my boss will understand when I tell him I'm needed in the US.* ('Needed' So pompous of me. But hey, in my defense, I was young and raring to go.)

"Okay, I can do that today," I nodded. "What else?"

"Well, let me see," he mused (or pretended to.) I say 'pretended to' as he had done this several times in the past. He knew all the requirements. "Then there's the visa."

"Visa?" I asked.

"Yes," he nodded. "Do you have a passport?" I nodded. "Good," he continued. "You have to go to the US Embassy. We'll give you a letter of employment and a letter from DBC. Do you own any property?"

I shook my head. The flat was in my father's name. "Is that going to be an issue?"

"It would have helped a lot. They want to see that you own something here to come back to. As it is, you don't have an advanced degree. You see, they want skilled workers with an advanced degree."

Suddenly, my shoulders drooped a little. I was feeling less confident now. I could hear the laughter of all the nerds who had buried their noses in the books, going religiously to the college library when I whiled my time at the Canteen. They had worked their butts off to get into a Master's or an Engineering program.

"Oh," I murmured, crestfallen a little now. He must have sensed it.

"Don't worry," he patted me on my back. You are not the first bachelor to go to the US. We have a 90% success rate with them getting a visa." If it meant to lift my mood, it wasn't helping. *But what about the 10%?* I was thinking. *What if I'm one of them?*

"Come back tomorrow," he continued, "I'll fill you in with the rest of the requirements."

Is there more? I panicked. "Okay," I nodded and turned around. I walked the rest of the hallway, wondering what the future held.

Chapter Four

The following day, I reached Mafatlal early. I had already called my boss and had tendered my resignation. And as I had expected, he was understanding of my need to be at my new place of work the next day.

"Don't worry," he had said, "I totally get it. You don't have to give your two weeks' notice."

Mr.V. was already waiting for me.

"Ah, there you are," he beckoned, "Come in."

I went to his office (cabin—as it's known in India) and sat in a chair across the table. He leaned forward and slid a piece of white paper across. I took it and started to read. It was an official letter of employment. *Phew,* I sighed to myself, feeling relieved. Why? Because I was unemployed as of yesterday; although, I had conveniently 'forgotten' to tell this to my family.

As I continued to scan through the document, my eyes were eagerly searching for a number. Ah, there it was. Rs.5,000/- (around $62) per month. That was more than double my current salary of Rs.2,000/- (around $25.)

I immediately signed the document and slid it back.

"Good," a satisfied smile spread across his face as he briefly scanned the document (probably to confirm that I had signed it.) "In addition to your Indian salary here, you will be getting a stipend of $1,000/- every month as your living expenses."

"Wow."

"Now, before you jump with joy, let me warn you that it's not much. But it's sufficient. Be frugal, don't splurge on unnecessary things. It will be highly tempting as you'll be seeing many attractive things. My advice to everyone who goes there is to think before you buy, ask yourself, 'do I NEED it or do I WANT it.' Don't eat out. Cook at home. Do you know how to?"

"No," I shook my head.

"Typical," he murmured under his breath. "Never mind," he continued a little louder, "but it's essential that you learn to cook, or else you'll end up doing the dishes."

"Huh?" I was confused.

"You see," he explained (I suspect he was enjoying this part), "most of the men we send don't know how to cook. And we house at least four a flat…er…apartment, start practicing the US lingo. So, if you know how to cook, you won't be able to contribute to the meal preparations. That means you'll end up doing the dishes, and trust me, you don't want to do that."

"No," I shook my head vigorously. "But I know how to cut vegetables. Doesn't that count as a contribution towards meal preparation?"

"Nice try, but no," he laughed. "I'd suggest you take a crash course in cooking before flying to the US."

"Yes," I nodded, "I'll do that." I made a mental note to learn how to cook. ABCDs, this may sound trivial to you guys, but it was a skill I had to master (okay, learn) along with my programming skills.

I started to get up from my chair. "Wait," he stopped me. "Yes?" I asked, halfway between the standing and sitting pose. "There's more, sit." he gestured. I plonked my butt back in the chair.

"Once you get your visa, you must go through our training course."

"Again?"

"No, no," he quickly shook his head. "This is a CAMP training course. You have to watch the training videos."

"What kind of videos? Don't you have any printed material I can take with me to study?"

"Yes, of course," he nodded. "You'll be given that too; however, in addition to the printed material, the videos consist of a series of lectures given by the person who developed CAMP. He explains in detail how the software works. It is something that no amount of printed material can replace. I strongly suggest you go through them in minute detail and try memorizing as much as possible."

"Believe me, you'll thank me." He got up from his chair, indicating the meeting was over. As I walked towards the door, he reminded me to collect the letter of employment and the letter from DBC from the receptionist.

*_*_*

I got up early the next day and reached the US Consulate on Warden Road (aka Breach Candy)[26] at 5 AM, thinking I'd be first in the queue. To my dismay, a long line had already formed. I suppose everyone had the same bright idea. I later discovered that the first person in the queue had stood there since 2 AM. I was crestfallen.

The consulate premises are surrounded by a tall wall prohibiting view. There's a bulletproof window on one side of the wall where a US sentry sits. Next to the window is an iron door to let people in. It opens at 9 AM, and they only allow a finite amount of people in. I didn't even know if they would let me in. If they didn't, I'd have to come the next day and try my luck again. *I should have been here at 3 AM,* I thought to myself. Looking at the long queue of hopeful faces, I knew I didn't stand a chance of being let in. I would have to come the next day. Suddenly, I heard a familiar voice calling me, "Hey, buddy." I looked around. The voice called again. I scanned the crowd to see where it was coming from. It was coming from the queue. A familiar face leaned out and waved at me. *Rajul!* I hurried to him and smiled. "You got in too?"

---

[26] Bhulabhai Desai Road, also well known by the old name Warden Road (and the part at and near the swimming pool as Breach Candy), is a niche up-market residential and semi-commercial locality of South Mumbai. Source: Wikipedia.

"Yes," he nodded, "come stand here." He didn't have to insist. I quickly (and very casually, so it looked like I was there for hours and stepped out to take a break) joined him. The person in front of us turned around and gave me a dirty look as if trying to say "who are you? You don't belong here; go to the back of the line."

"When did you get here?" I asked Rajul softly, ensuring the man in front of us couldn't hear us.

"3 AM."

I looked at him and merely shook my head in disbelief.

"Do you know who else got in?" I asked.

"Rahul," he smiled, and then he looked at his wristwatch, "He should have been here a long time ago. That idiot promised me last evening that he'd be here by 3:30-4:00." Just then, we saw Rahul hurrying towards us. "Sorry, *yaar*."

"What happened? Where were you?" Rajul asked.

"Didn't get a bus for a very long time; had to take a taxi."

The man in front turned around again, looking angry this time. "How many of you are there?"

"Just us three," Rajul replied. "Anyways, sir, it shouldn't impact you as you are ahead of us."

"Oh," the man's facial expressions changed from anger to a sheepish grin. "Right." He turned back to his family.

"*Chai garam* (hot tea)," a voice yelled. A boy was walking with a kettle in one hand and a stack of glasses in the other. Every now and then, a person standing in the queue would stop him and stick out several fingers to tell him how many he wanted. The boy then would pour (with flair) a steaming glass of tea and hand it to the person.

```
<Begin rant>

Tea in Hindi is chai. So, you young hipsters,
when I hear you guys saying, 'I like Chai Tea,' I
just want to pull at my remaining hair. Please do
the cultural appropriation right. I'd be very
proud and happy to hear 'I like Chai.'

</End rant>
```

"Do you want some?" Rajul asked.

"No," I shook my head, fearing that drinking tea would start a chain reaction in my intestine, and there was no toilet facility to be seen anywhere around where we were.

We discussed our interviews and the salary packages we were offered (we were all offered the same package.)

```
<Begin confession>

It was pervasive (back then, at least. I don't
know if it's a no-no now) to ask someone "how
much do you make?"
People in the US freak out when someone asks them
the value of their house. Newsflash, people:
There's something called Zillow now. What you
paid is not a big secret. Anyone with an internet
connection can find out.

</End confession>
```

Eventually, the queue started to move. The decibel level of the anticipated murmur rose. I finally saw what the building looked like. I had passed the consulate hundreds of times but could never actually see the building as it was hidden behind the tall walls.

Aerial view

Ground view

We walked into the building and were directed to the interview room. I eagerly entered the room. It was a big room with blue walls. Portraits of the current president and vice-president flanked the US flag. A blue carpet covered the floor. A circular emblem of the US Consulate that showed the American bald eagle with its wings spread ran a few feet apart from one another, all the way from one end to the other. Rows of plastic chairs faced a glass enclosure divided into small cubicles. The interviewer would occupy one side of the booth; the interviewee sat on the other side. A thick (probably bulletproof) glass separated them.

Having been in this country for over thirty years now and having seen many shows on TV, it now reminds me of a prison visitors' area, where the loved ones and the prisoner talk to each other on a phone while a glass separates them. The only difference was that we didn't have phones.

<Begin confession>

Actually, it's more like a bank teller. In fact, it very much resembles that. The ones you see in prisons probably are thin plexiglass, whereas these were thick and bulletproof.

I'm just dramatizing it to make it sound juicier.

</End confession>

On top of each cubicle, a red neon sign displayed the number. Soon, my number was called. I took a deep breath and got up from my chair.

"Good luck," Rajul said.

"Thanks," I mumbled weakly. I went up to the cubicle. A lady in her forties was sitting on the other side of the glass enclosure.

"Papers, please?" she thrust out a hand. I handed her the visa form, along with my other two letters. She took them from me and scanned them. I held my breath.

"Do you have any other documents?" She looked up at me for the first time.

"No, miss," I shook my head. I was coached by Mr. V. to address them as miss.

"It lists the residential address on your form. Is it a property?"

"Yes," I nodded enthusiastically, "it's a flat."

"Is it in your name?" she looked at me over her glasses.

"No, my father owns it."

"So," she looked at the form again. "In other words, you don't own anything here."

"Y—yes," I mumbled. My throat had turned dry.

"Hmm," she contemplated for what seemed like an eternity. "Well," she finally said, "I usually deny such visas."

"Oh," I croaked hoarsely. I was crestfallen. She looked at my sad face. She looked at the form again, trying to decide her next move. She could either make my dreams come true by granting a visa or put the US as a distant country that would be out of my reach.

She looked at me and smiled, "tell you what, I'll make an exception in your case. I'll grant you a US visa for six months."

"Thank you very much," I gave her a silly grin, forgetting the miss part Mr.V. had taught me. I felt an enormous weight being lifted off of my shoulders.

```
<Begin confession>

I'll never forget the lady who changed my life.
Thank you…oops…thank you, miss.

</End confession>
```

Soon, it was Rahul's turn. He, too, was granted a visa. Unfortunately, Rajul had to come the next day with some additional documents. He was then given the visa.

I had now crossed one of the hurdles. There were two more to go. I was not worried about one of them as I just had to watch videos. However, the other one made me more nervous. I had to learn how to cook (those who know how to, stop laughing and those who don't, sympathize.)

I called my family from a pay phone and gave them the good news. "Congratulations!" my wife said.

"Thank you, but…."

"But, what?" she sensed my hesitation.

"There is a small problem." I didn't want to admit that it was a big issue.

"What is it?"

"Can I talk to *Mummy?*" My mother came on the line. "Hello, *beta* (son)."

"You have to teach me how to cook," I exclaimed.

"What?" she sounded confused.

"I have to learn how to cook."

"Why?" She was intrigued.

"I'll explain everything to you when I come home."

"Okay."

After saying goodbye, I hung up the phone. I shook my head as I visualized her and my wife having a good laugh at my expense.

We: Rahul, Rajul, and I decided to celebrate with a chilled beer the next day after Rajul got his visa.

I caught the 84Exp. to head home.

--*

When I reached home, my wife greeted me with a big smile. "So, you want to learn how to cook." The smirk, along with the mischievous twinkle in those beautiful eyes. I could see that she was enjoying this.

"Yes," I nodded sheepishly.

"Why?" she asked. I explained my reason, and she got

it. "I see," she smiled, "don't you wish you had *Pappaji's* skills?"

"Yes," I rolled my eyes. My father was the only male in our family who knew how to cook. My brother and I knew nothing (well, not nothing. We knew how to boil water.)

I went into the kitchen, where my mother was already busy.

"Ah, *jaldi aavi gayo* (you came pretty soon.)"

"Yes, opposite direction," I said. We lived in the suburbs of Mumbai. The morning rush hour traffic would be in the direction of downtown.

"Come," she beckoned as she stirred the vegetables being cooked on the cooking range (we call it gas.)

She opened a drawer and took out a circular, stainless steel container, and opened it. Curiously, I looked in the mysterious box. I had seen it before when I was rummaging through the kitchen drawers (looking for a beer bottle opener) but had always ignored it, dismissing it as 'not-what-I-want .' However, it was different from that time. I wanted it; rather, I *needed* it. It consisted of small circular containers. They all were neatly arranged to fit in a concentric circle. They all contained different colored, textured spices and seeds: yellow turmeric (culturally appropriated and sold as a supplemental drug here), red chili powder, mustard seeds, brownish-green coriander powder, cumin seeds, cinnamon sticks, cloves, cardamoms, and so on. The familiar aroma of several Indian dishes filled my nostrils.

"These are the basic spices," she explained, "there are many more for you to master in a few days. But I just want you to learn the basics of Indian cooking today. When making our basic vegetables (ours was a vegetarian household), you must know the simple things first.

```
<Begin Indian vegetarian definition>
```

```
The term 'Vegan' was not invented back then. Our
household was 'eggetarian,' which means that we
(my brother and I) used to eat omelets at home. I
am a Hindu, and my wife is a Jain (strictly
vegetarian.) In fact, many Jains refrain from
eating anything that grows under the ground. That
means no potatoes, onions, garlic, carrots, etc.
```

```
Yes, they practice their beliefs here too. I
remember, many years ago, when we were new to
this country, our daughter attended Sunday school
to learn about the Indian religion of Jainism.
One day she returned home and informed me that
she didn't want to be Jain anymore because she
loved garlic, and Jainism forbade eating anything
made with garlic.
```

```
</End Indian vegetarian definition>
```

"Let's start with the easiest. Make a potato dish. I've already boiled, peeled, and cut them." She took out a new pan, put it on the cooking range, and turned the knob on. She then poured oil into it. She opened the drawer, took out a small plastic bottle, and added a pinch of the powder.

"What's that?" I asked, alarmed, as this was not part of the circular container.

"*Hing* (asafoetida)[27]," she explained. She proceeded to throw in a few dried curry leaves. As they hit the oil, they started to welt and sizzle. Next, she reached for the round container (finally) and expertly added a tiny spoonful of mustard seed, cumin seeds, red chili powder, and turmeric powder. She started stirring them together. The familiar aroma of Indian dishes wafted through the kitchen, and my mouth started to drool. When the sizzling sound of mustard and cumin seeds became sporadic, she tilted the plate containing potatoes in. As they smoothly slid in, the sizzle picked up once again. She started to mix them.

I extended a hand and opened my palm. "Let me do it." She handed me the flat ladle. I slowly and nervously started mixing the potatoes, ensuring I wouldn't spill any. A grin slowly spread across my face. "I can do this," I said cockily.

"Really?" my wife raised her eyebrows. "So, you think you can cook now, huh?" I looked at her and nodded.

"What about the other things?"

"What other things?" my smile faded.

"There's *roti*[28] and *daal*[29]. Are you just planning to eat

---

[27] In Indian English, hing is a sticky liquid with a strong smell that is obtained from the roots of certain plants. The English word is asafoetida. Source: Collins Hindi-English dictionary.

[28] Roti (also known as chapati) is a round flatbread native to the Indian subcontinent. Source: Wikipedia.

[29] In Indian cuisine, dal (also spelled daal or dhal) are dried, split pulses (e.g., lentils, peas, and beans) that do not require soaking before cooking. India is the largest producer of pulses in

vegetables?"

I groaned. I felt overwhelmed.

```
<Begin confession>

I realize now that there's so much being done
just to put three basic things on my plate. And
as you all know, Indian cooking is not limited to
three things, nor is it limited to a particular
cuisine. Each state and region in India has its
own method of cooking. Most Indian restaurants
abroad just serve one type of cuisine—Mughlai
cuisine³⁰.

I salute all the Indian moms and wives who toiled
for hours in the kitchen to feed their sons,
daughters, and husbands.

</End confession>
```

To really understand and appreciate a broad spectrum of
Indian food, I urge my non-Indian friends to attend an

---

the world. The term is also used for various soups prepared from
these pulses. These pulses are among the most important staple
foods in South Asian countries, and form an important part of
the cuisines of the Indian subcontinent. Source: Wikipedia.

[30] Mughlai cuisine consists of dishes developed in
the medieval Indo-Persian cultural centres of the Mughal Empire. It
represents a combination of cuisine of the Indian subcontinent with
the cooking styles and recipes of Central Asian and Islamic cuisine.
Mughlai cuisine is strongly influenced by the Turkic cuisine
of Central Asia, the region where the early Mughal
emperors originally hailed from, and it has in turn strongly
influenced the regional cuisines of Northern
India, Pakistan and Bangladesh. Source: Wikipedia.

Indian wedding or go to a potluck (if they get a chance.) I promise you that a whole new world will open up to you.

"I'm sure *rotis* are available in the store there," my mother said. "And as far as *daal* is concerned, I'll teach that to you tomorrow."

"Okay, *Mummy*," I nodded. "Thanks."

"What thanks? *Bahu aavyo thanks kehevawalo.* (Loosely translated, no thanks required." I say loosely, not literally, since the literal translation may sound ridiculous. Almost all languages have several ways of saying things that lose their underlying essence when translated to English (or any other language.) Case in point, try reading the English subtitles of a Bollywood movie. If you know Hindi, you'll find them utterly ridiculous. However, they make a lot of sense to others.

```
<Begin rant>

Hey Bollywood, stop subtitling songs. Some of the
translations border on sheer vulgarity.

</End rant>
```

My mother busied herself in preparing the *roti* and *daal.* I've never had a more delicious lunch before. I took an extra serving of my 'masterpiece.'

```
<Begin confession>

I now realize how tiny my contribution really
was.

</End confession>
```

A typical *masala dabba* (spice container) found in all Indian kitchens

Chapter Five

Having crossed two hurdles (although I still was under the watchful tutelage of my mother and my wife for the second hurdle—cooking), I had one more hurdle to cross: training.

Soon, our training started. In addition to memorizing the printed material that Mr. V. had given us, we were required to watch a series of lectures on a video. Rajul, Rahul, and I huddled around a 32-inch television and inserted the first cassette into the VHS video player (VHS —short for Video Home System—is a standard for consumer-level analog video recording on tape cassettes) on top of the television. Rajul took control of the remote and hit play. We eagerly looked at the screen. After a few seconds of static, an image appeared. A man was standing in front of a whiteboard. He was pointing to the writing.

"This is the style inquiry screen," he pointed his Sharpie to the whiteboard. *He looks familiar,* I thought.

"You have Style, Style-suffix, Color, Color-suffix, and Location," he tapped through the neatly scribbled writings. However, I wasn't paying attention to what he was saying; instead, I was sifting through my brain. *Where have I seen him?* Not being able to identify the face was killing me. Just then, a white subtitle gently scrolled through. Narayan Murthy.

My eyes widened; Narayana *Murthy? The Narayana Murthy?* Who's he? I'd say that he's Bill Gates of India. A quick Google search will tell you that: N.R. Narayana Murthy is an Indian billionaire businessman. He is the founder of Infosys and has been the chairman, chief executive officer (CEO), president, and chief mentor of the company before retiring and taking the title of chairman emeritus. As of April 2022, his net worth was estimated at US$4.4 billion. He, along with <u>five others</u>, founded Infosys in 1981. It started with a capital of US$250 and now has become a US$ 104.71 billion company. Traded in NYSE, it employs over 310,000 professionals and has a global presence. He also happens to be the father-in-law of the British PM, Rishi Sunak.

Back in 1978, when Donn Liles came to India for the first time, Narayana Murthy was working for Patni Computers. He then developed CAMP for Donn Liles to run on Data General machines. A few years after that, with Donn Liles' encouragement, he founded Infosys and ported CAMP from Data General to IBM Mainframes.

In 2004, Donn Liles was <u>honored in a ceremony by Infosys to show their appreciation</u>. (I keep saying to myself that *someone should make a documentary on this.*)

After an hour or so, our initial excitement wore off.

Rajul began to fast forward the tape, and we didn't stop him.

```
<Begin confession>

We didn't see the entire recording. Sorry, Donn.

</End confession>
```

After a few days, we had completed our 'training.' We had to pretend that we saw the videos in their entirety. Obviously, we couldn't go to Mr.V. the next day and report that we had seen all the videos. However, we were not very confident in our knowledge of CAMP. We feared being exposed. *What if someone asks a CAMP-related question?* I panicked. This invariably led me down the rabbit hole of doom and gloom.

*_*_*

Soon, it was time to leave. I busied myself by putting things together to pack. Mafatlal had booked us on Kuwait Airways. We were scheduled to fly in fifteen days. We were allowed two suitcases to carry with us. I looked at the pile of clothes I wanted to take. That was when reality hit me. How can I pack over two decades of life in merely two suitcases? Besides, Mumbai is a tropical city with a hot climate and humidity. I had never worn a sweater (let alone a winter coat) in my life. Mr.V. had given us a list of things we would need during winter. I opened the list, and my heart sank as I started going through the items. Gloves, muffler, woolen socks, sturdy shoes, a warm coat, beanies (I didn't know what it was), a thick sweater,…I stopped. It was too overwhelming. This list was only for winter clothes. I still had to carry my regular attire. In addition to the clothes, I had to take the essential ingredients to cook an Indian meal. People who had already been to the US had advised me to carry Indian snacks. "You won't be allowed to take fruits and vegetables, so don't even bother packing them. The customs officers will throw it away."

"Oh, and by the way, make sure you see the other side of the road before crossing. Unlike here, they drive on the other side. While driving, if you ever get pulled over, do not, under any circumstances, I repeat, do not get out of the car and approach the officer. He'll think you are trying to attack him and will draw a gun on you. Remember, it's a gun culture, so you'll see lots of guns. And don't even think about trying to bribe an officer of the law. He will arrest you and throw you in jail." All these were highly valuable tips; however, they had the exact opposite effect. It was terrifying. I began to doubt leaving my beloved country where I fit in.

"When you have to go visit someone, just don't show up unannounced. Call them in advance and see if they are available. Even Indians don't appreciate this. Respect their privacy, and know your boundaries. You'll see lots of different-looking people. Do not stare. It's considered highly rude," and the barrage of advice continued.

<Begin confession>

"How will I take all this stuff?" I groaned.

"Don't worry," my mother said, "just carry the most important things you'll require."

"What about this list?" I showed her the winter clothes list given to me by Mr.V.

"Let me have a look," my brother thrust his hand. I handed it to him, and he scanned through it. "Ah," he exclaimed.

"What?" I asked.

"You don't have to take a single thing from this."

"Why not?"

"This is April. You'll be there at the beginning of the summer season. You won't be needing any of these for a while. You'll have enough time to look for a bargain there," he smiled.

"Oh, right." I felt as if an enormous weight was lifted off of my shoulders. I started to feel better. I busied myself with packing the suitcase.

```
</End confession>
```

Then there was the question of money. As I told you earlier, I come from a middle-class family. I was conscious of the fact that I could not expect a lot of it from my parents. My brother had not yet started his new job. I had just joined Mafatlal, so to ask them for an advance was out of the question. I didn't want to ask my wife, although she would have willingly and happily given whatever she had.

```
<Begin confession>

When I was dating my wife, most of the time, I
was kadka (without money.) Over five years of
dating, there have been innumerable occasions
where she has paid the bill.

</End confession>
```

I went to my father. "*Pappaji.*"

"Yes," he looked up from the book he was reading.

"I'll need some cash," I mumbled.

"Of course, I'll get some from the bank tomorrow." He went back to his book. *I hope he knows I meant dollars*, I thought. However, I didn't want to tell him that. I'll ask *mummy* to let him know. I always used her as a go-between me and *pappaji*. If I wanted a new ball to play cricket, ask *mummy*. Ask mummy if I wanted a pair of new shoes to attend a karate camp. She then would tell *pappaji*. I knew he made the final decision and rarely said no (almost never). However, this arrangement of a relay game worked well.

"Why don't you ask him directly? You're a married man now," my wife would say.

"You don't understand."

"What is there to understand?" I would always ask my dad.

"That's different. *Pappaji* is not your dad."

She would continue to goad me until we changed the subject.

Packing was almost over. The suitcases were already filled to the top. My wife flipped the covers and zipped them shut (while my brother and I sat on them to press the contents.)

"Careful, don't put too much pressure," my mother warned me. "There are fragile things that can get damaged."

I lifted the suitcase a few inches from the ground to feel its weight. It felt heavy. I asked my brother to slide the weighing scale below it. I gently rested it on the scale and looked at the rotating numbers until they stopped. All of us were holding our breaths. We heaved a collective sigh when the number stopped on the allowable weight limit. We repeated the same with the other suitcase.

Fortunately, it, too, was right on the dot.

"Good," I clapped, "No more adding."

"But, what about the stuff you have to carry for others?" my mother protested.

"I'm not taking it. Tell them the bags were full, so he couldn't take it."

"They will be disappointed."

"I know, but I have a solution."

"What?"

"Tell them I'm more than happy to carry their stuff provided they pay for the extra baggage," I laughed. "See, problem solved."

Chapter Six

Sahar International Airport (Renamed in 1999 from 'Sahar Airport' to 'Chhatrapati Shivaji Maharaj International Airport') is one of the busiest airports in India. Back then, there was the old structure that is decommissioned now. The new facility adjacent to it started its operations in February of 2014.

I was greeted by a cacophony of passengers, their loved ones, airport staff, hawkers, policemen, etc. Unlike post-9/11, all of us (not just the travelers) were allowed to enter the building. There were rows of shiny plastic seats that were joined together with an iron rod running through its base. The white linoleum floor shone with the reflection of bright ceiling lights.

My family and my childhood friends had come to see me off. I saw Rajul and Rahul, too, surrounded by their respective loved ones. It was easy to identify who was flying as a bright red tika marked them[31] on their foreheads. In addition to this, many travelers also had garlands around their necks. They looked highly uncomfortable in the Mumbai heat. Although my mother would have preferred to have one around my neck, I had warned my mother that I would entertain no such ritual. I was supported by my father, my brother, and my wife.

"Leave the poor boy alone," my father had said. "Don't torture him in this heat." Finally, reluctantly, she had relented. However, she had fussed over me at my house by applying *tilak* and doing my *aarti*.

```
<Begin rant>

If you look up the definition of aarti on
Wikipedia, it's defined as a Hindu religious
ritual of worship, often part of puja (prayer),
in which light (usually from a flame) is offered
to one or more deities.
Aarti(s) also refers to the songs sung to praise
the deity when the light is offered.

Now you tell me, how in the hell can I be
worshiped? When I was younger, I always used to
question the reason behind the rituals. I would
find many of them ridiculous. However, I've
learned over the years that logic and religious
rituals don't go together. I generally accept it
if it's something that's not causing me any harm.
```

---

[31] In Dharmic culture, the tilaka is a mark worn usually on the forehead. Historically, tilaka were also used in other Dharmic cultures including Buddhism, Jainism and Sikhism, which were influenced by Hinduism and its spiritual and philosophical beliefs. Source: Wikipedia.

Moreover, India is deeply immersed in its traditions that go back thousands of years. Each state, religion, and culture has its own idiosyncrasies. So, the message is unmistakable — Take it or leave it, but for heaven's sake, stop arguing.

I've always found this to be true across religions worldwide.

</End rant>

I went to the airline's counter to check in my luggage. I handed the young lady behind the counter my ticket (yes, we only had paper tickets back then). I placed my suitcases (one after another) on the weighing scale and held my breath in nervous anticipation. I was afraid of the bags being over the allowed weight limit. I would have to open them and take out things if they were. I started to recollect the things that could be discarded mentally and came up with nothing. Everything was essential for me to start a new life in a foreign land. Fortunately, none of them were above the limit. The lady expertly printed the baggage tags and wrapped them around the handles. She then asked the luggage handler to place my suitcases on the conveyor belt. I saw them disappear into the mysterious internals of the loading system.

<Begin confession>

I've always found the complexities of loading the baggage on the right plane fascinating. To me, it's just a mysterious black hole where my luggage disappears. It probably is not so

mysterious when I find out how the internals
work.

As you can tell, I'm curious about how things
work. Maybe it's my science background.

If I find something fascinating, I tend to forget
about everything. My wife will attest to it. I
remember when I got my hands on a Commodore 64[32].
In 1983, a friend visited the US and brought it
back. When I went to see him, he showed me that.
It was love at first sight. I was so fascinated
by it that I spent the next two hours playing
with it, completely forgetting I was supposed to
call my wife (we had begun dating very recently,
thus the initial excitement phase.) To this day,
I feel guilty about that cardinal sin.

</End confession>

Like all the flights that departed with the US as their
final destination, my flight to Kuwait was in the middle of
the night. Hence, it was way past bedtime for all who had
come to the airport. A mixture of excitement and sadness
hung in the air. I saw a big smile on everyone's face, but I
also sensed a little bit of sadness. They all were rooting
for me to make my life, but at the same time, were sad to
see me go.

<Begin confession>

----

[32] The Commodore 64, also known as the C64 or the CBM 64, is
an 8-bit home computer introduced in January 1982
by Commodore International (first shown at the Consumer
Electronics Show, January 7–10, 1982, in Las Vegas). Source:
Wikipedia.

```
All my friends are from my childhood. In addition
to being from the same neighborhood, we also went
to the same school. Even now, after so many
years, whenever I visit India, there never is an
awkward pause in our conversation. I feel as if I
met them yesterday.
```

```
</End confession>
```

Soon, it was time for me to depart. The melodious voice announced the initial boarding for my flight. I touched my parents' feet (an Indian ritual to show respect towards the elders) and hugged every one of them. I could see that my wife was fighting tears while she put on a brave smile. We ambled to the security checkpoint, me tightly holding my wife's hand. Rahul and Rajul did the same.

I crossed the barrier that said, 'ONLY PASSENGERS ALLOWED.' A police officer checked my passport and boarding card before letting me through. My loved ones crowded around the steel railings. I walked towards the security gate that would let me enter the immigration area. At the entrance, I turned around. I saw my loved ones waving at me. I waved back, fighting tears. I turned around and went through the gate.

Little did I imagine that I would not see them for the next three years. I was twenty-five-year-old and had USD$400.

*_*_*

We went through the tunnel that connected the airplane

with the structure. A smiling stewardess greeted us at the door of the plane. After checking the seat numbers on our boarding passes, she pointed toward the aircraft's right. We walked through the aisle to reach our seats. They were at the back of the plane, the very last ones, next to the restrooms.

```
<Begin confession>

I had never flown in a plane before. Hence, I had
no clue how the seat assignments worked. Little
did I know that the last seats didn't tilt
backward. Nor did I realize our close proximity
to the restrooms. A long queue of passengers
would soon form to empty their bowels, especially
after the food was served.

I say 'flown' as I had seen the inside of an
airplane before. When I was in school, my
neighbor—who worked at the airport—had taken my
family to see the Jumbo Jet when it first arrived
at Mumbai airport. This was in 1971.

</End confession>
```

I looked at my fellow travelers and imitated them fastening their seat belts. Soon, I felt a jerk as the plane was thrust backward from its gate. Eventually, it started to move forward, making its way through the runway to the main landing and takeoff strip. I looked out the window to see the buildings passing in the opposite direction.

When it was our turn to take off, I felt a thrust. My body was pressed to the back of the seat as the airplane gathered momentum. When it reached its desired speed, it lifted off gently. I felt as though my stomach had dropped. I could immediately hear the motors churning as the tires receded in the belly of the plane. The three of us looked at one another, trying to give a hollow smile. However, each one had a glum face. The excitement of going to the US had been replaced by the reality of the unknown that lay ahead.

I lit a cigarette, and Rajul did the same (yes, we could smoke on a plane back then.) We had reserved our seats in a smoking section (as if the smoke we blew out would know how to restrict itself in the smoking section).

```
<Begin confession>

Looking back, I realize how ridiculous the whole
concept of the smoking and non-smoking section
was. My apologies to all the nonsmokers subjected
to second-hand inhalation of toxic fumes.

</End confession>
```

Soon, the meal was served. The aroma of the food trays being reheated wafted through the plane. Somewhere in the front rows, someone had unwrapped *theplas*[33]. The familiar scent whisked me back to Kripa Nagar. I could visualize my parents enjoying them as breakfast. It was a daily ritual for them to have *theplas* with hot coffee.

---

[33] Thepla is a soft Indian flatbread typical of Gujarati cuisine
It is typically enjoyed as a breakfast, or can be eaten for snacks.It can also be served as a side dish with a meal, or as a snack in the late afternoon. Source: Wikipedia.

Although I had taken them for granted in the past, I suddenly craved *theplas*. I started to miss my family.

```
<Begin confession>

Theplas can be aromatic to some while offensive
to others, particularly to those who have not
been exposed to them. To many Indians, especially
Gujaratis, they are not only satiating but
unlocking memories. I've found it to be more true
in the US (and I'm sure it's so in the other
countries). They take them back to their fond
memories of their time in India.

</End confession>
```

We, Rahul, Rajul, and I, were too anxious to eat our meals. The stewardess took the untouched tray back and momentarily reappeared to serve coffee and tea (which we happily drank, along with smoking more cigarettes.)

I looked up at the small screen above the frame to the other section. It displayed the route our plane would take. My eyes were drawn to a small arrow in the bottom-right corner. It was pointing upwards and was slightly tilted to the right. *What is it?* I wondered. I asked Rajul and Rahul, but both of them too were mystified. Just then, the stewardess passed us. "Excuse me, miss," I said loudly. She stopped and turned around. "Yes."

"What is that for?" I pointed at the screen, "the arrow."

"Oh, that. That shows the direction of Mecca. It helps Muslims face it when they pray." Soon, the arrow shifted to the left. It was now pointing upwards.

Suddenly, I hear a man shout. Startled, I looked behind.

Ours was the last row, but behind us was a narrow passageway connecting the two aisles. I see a turbaned man with a thick beard. He was wearing a white robe. He had covered his ears with his palms. He was doing his *namaz* (Muslim prayers). Many passengers, too, were startled by the commotion, while others were unfazed. They were used to seeing this on a plane. Kuwait Airways belonging to a Muslim country was extremely accommodating to a Muslim's needs.

Remember, this was pre-9/11. I'm sure these Middle-eastern airlines have since modified their rules to be more sensitive to others' needs.

```
<Begin pre-9/11>

9/11 has changed airline travel. Once, before
9/11, I was flying back to Mumbai via Lufthansa.
I requested the air hostess to allow me to
witness the plane landing from the cockpit. To my
pleasant surprise, I was ushered to the cockpit,
where the pilot asked me to sit behind him and
wear headphones so that I could hear the
conversation between the plane and the air
traffic control. It was a mesmerizing experience
that I'll remember for the rest of my life.

The 9/11 terrorists robbed this from many (like
me) who just wanted to experience a plane
landing.

</End pre-9/11>
```

After the four-hour flight to Kuwait, we had a layover, where we changed planes and braced ourselves for the fourteen-hour haul to New York.

* * *

```
<Begin confession>

Since it was my first plane ride, fourteen hours
didn't sound that bad. However, when I look back,
I shudder whenever I think about it. However,
it's two hours shorter than the sixteen-hour
nonstop flight I take now from Los Angeles to
Dubai.

</End confession>
```

Finally, the activities picked up as we neared our destination. Eventually, I heard the familiar noise of the motors as the tires lowered themselves from the plane's belly. I felt the bottom of my stomach drop as the plane lowered. After a few judders and shakes, I lurched as the tires touched the runway. The engines reversed to recede the speed. I gulped hard. My ears popped to adjust the altitude.

I was in the US of A.

From Vada Pavs to Hotdogs

I ate the homemade curry,
and flew to the glamour-land.
A new charm, some new worries
but a strong faith in fate's hand.
I wondered what was in store
as my dreams fluttered in hope.
Knocking on destiny's door
with an iron will to cope.
Joy or woe of the new dough-
Alas! little did I know.

Chapter Seven

I peered out of the window. I was fascinated to see the building, workers in their bright yellow vests with walkie-talkies hanging around their waists, going about their respective duties. Different shaped, colored, and sized vehicles were running about haphazardly.

The stewardess announced that the passengers should stay seated with their seat belts fastened until the captain had switched off the seat belt sign. We all eagerly looked at it as the plane slowed down and came to a complete halt. We heard the seat belt sign go off with a ding. Immediately, chaos ensued as all the passengers got up from their seats and opened the overhead compartments to collect their carry-on belongings. We, the three of us, didn't have any. And since we were in the very last row, we remained seated, checking (and double-checking) our passports and immigration forms.

Finally, the crowd thinned as the passengers made their way to exit the plane. When it was our turn, we too got up and followed them, passing empty rows of seats (all messy now) as we made our way through the aisle. The pleasant stewardess flashed a radiating smile as we alighted. "Thank you for flying with us; come again."

All the gates were occupied; hence our plane had stopped on the tarmac. Instead of making our way up the tunnel, we walked into a rectangular compartment with windows. It made a low humming sound as the air-conditioner cooled it. Gingerly, we stood in the compartment and held on to the overhead handles. As soon as the last passenger had walked through, a light started flashing with a beeping sound. The door behind us was slowly sliding down. When it shut completely, the beeping stopped. Momentarily, we felt a lurch. As I looked out of the window, I saw the aircraft rising. In actuality, we were lowering. Finally, the compartment stopped with a hiss. I looked around. We were on the ground level. The beeping began once more. We felt a lurch. We were moving forward.

It was a specially made feeder-bus capable of raising its compartment to align it to the aircraft's door to collect passengers. It then would take the passengers to the terminal. It was deployed when all the terminal gates were occupied, and the arriving flight had to park on the tarmac.

<Begin confession>

I had never seen such a contraption before in my life; I thought it was an ingenious idea to carry many passengers without making them climb down (especially those passengers who had difficulty climbing down the stairs) the plane and walk to

83

the bus. That was my very first exposure to
American ingenuity, and my feet had not even
touched US soil. Well thought.

</End confession>

The feeder bus navigated its way, weaving through the
bustling activities. It finally stopped. The beep again
started, and the door slid upwards. We walked into a
broad passageway with shiny floors and blue walls. Large
photos of famous American monuments adorned them.
On the other end of the corridor were large doors.
Portraits of the current US President and Vice-President
smiled with their hands folded. They flanked a sign with
the words, "Welcome to America."

As we walked through the doors, the decibel level of
people chattering had picked up. I looked around in awe.
We were standing in a vast area. Multiple queues of
passengers were awaiting their turn at the immigration
counter, where an immigration officer sat in a blue
uniform. Behind the counter, the police officers (also in
their traditional blue uniforms) stood with their arms
akimbo. A utility belt was tied around their waists,
housing a gun, a pair of handcuffs, and a flashlight. A
shiny badge was pinned on their chests. A small walkie-
talkie was snugly tied to their shoulders, allowing them to
communicate with their hands free. Their faces were
stolid, devoid of any facial expression. Their eyes scanned
the passengers.

* * *

I had never seen so many people from different countries and cultures. People with various features, skin tones, and attire. The cacophony was a mixture of multiple languages spoken. I strained my ears to pick up any Indian languages I knew and was rewarded by some familiar sound.

Soon, I was in the front of the queue. I heard a voice. "Next, please." I felt Rajul's palm on the small of my back. "Go," he gently nudged me. I crossed the yellow line (we were supposed to stand behind it until we were called.) I adjusted my shirt, smiled widely, and walked to the counter. An African-American lady was sitting behind the counter.

from one of the African countries when I used to
visit my friends at his college campus when he
was studying for their Master's degree. They
always looked exotic to me, with their dark skins
glistening in the sweltering Mumbai heat.

</End confession>

She thrust a hand and opened her palm while continuing to look at the screen in front of her. I handed her my passport and the immigration form. She briefly scanned it, her eyes darting from the photo to my face, comparing and verifying. When she was satisfied, she placed it on a scanning device. I saw my image getting rasterized on the screen. Next, she studied the immigration form and verified it with the duration of my visa.

"Purpose of your visit?" she asked.

"Business," I replied nervously.

"Hmm," she frowned, concentrating on the form. Finally, when she was satisfied that everything was in order, she stamped the form, tore a portion, and stapled it on my passport. "Make sure to return it when you leave."

"Okay," I nodded. She handed back my passport. "Thank you," I smiled, but she wasn't listening. She was already calling Rajul, "Next."

<Begin confession>

Although I grew up in Mumbai and have watched
many Hollywood movies, I was hoping that she
wouldn't ask me any more questions, as I'm sure I
would not have understood what she was saying.

</End confession>

* * *

I walked to the rows of empty luggage carts, took one, and wheeled it to the carousel belt to collect my suitcases, ensuring that the sign flashed Kuwait Airways. There were rows of carousel belts. Each one of them showed a sign of a different airline flashing. New York's John F. Kennedy airport is one of the busiest airports in the world, serving millions of passengers arriving on other airlines. Each carousel belt had a chute in the middle. It spat out pieces of luggage and onto the rotating carousel. Various shaped, sized, and colored suitcases now lazily rotated around. I craned my neck to identify mine and was eventually able to spot it. As it came to me, I quickly picked it up and placed it on the cart. Fortunately, both my suitcases were next to one another, so I could quickly collect them. Both Rajul and Rahul did the same, and the three of us headed to the signboard which said, 'Customs Inspection.' Since none of us had any perishables (Thank you, Mr.V., for giving us strict instructions that we were not to carry them,) we breezed through the green channel (that means 'nothing to declare.')

We wheeled our carts and were greeted by a crowd of hundreds of eager faces who had come to receive their loved ones.

"There he is," Rahul said when he spotted the man.

Mr.S. (name withheld) had come to receive us. He was a

portly South Indian man in his fifties with a slight belly, a thick mustache, and salt-n-pepper straight hair that was neatly combed. He wore a gray jacket over a blue tee shirt and black trousers. White Pumas contrasted the color of his pants.

Our expressions must have shown the relief to see a familiar face. "Hi," he smiled. I had first met Mr.S. at Mafatlal after my interview. When I entered the reception area, he was talking to the lady behind the desk.

"This is not my first visit to New York," he was saying. I gathered that he, too, would be joining DBC; however, I'd not seen him taking the course. I introduced myself. We started talking. He informed me that he had been interviewed by Donn earlier that morning and was already selected. And since this would not be his first trip to the US, he already had a multiple-entry visa. I was impressed and a little envious.

"So, you will be programming with us, huh? That's wonderful; we can learn from your experience."

"*Nahi, re* (No, man)," he smiled as he shook his head, "I won't be programming. I'm hired as a manager."

I hid my disappointment. "Oh, I see." It then dawned on me that he would be my boss. "Will I be working under you?"

He shrugged, "I don't know, but most likely. I'll be overseeing all the programmers in New York, which means it's more than possible that I'll be overseeing you too."

"That's wonderful," I said enthusiastically, but I was

careful not to sound too eager. I didn't want to be misunderstood. I, however, was feeling relieved that there would be an Indian buffer between Donn and me. I was a little apprehensive about communicating with him daily, fearing that I would blunder as I was not very confident in my English (remember, ETL—English as a Third language or EFL—English as a Fourth Language?) Mr.S. then proceeded to give me some valuable tips on the visa interview and life in America and promised to receive me at the airport if I got my visa.

Now, seeing him in front of me, I was relieved to see a familiar face.

"Come," he guided us to the exit, and we followed him, gawking in awe at our surroundings. We hailed two yellow taxis. Sure, we all could fit in one; however, we needed the second taxi to fit our suitcases. There was no way to fit six oversized bags in one. So, two of us rode in the front cab, and the other two followed us. I jumped at the opportunity to ride with Mr.S. in the front vehicle.

```
<Begin confession>

Sorry, Rahul and Rajul, for making you feel
abandoned, even if it was for a brief while.

</End confession>
```

As the taxi sped towards our destination with the driver regularly glancing in the rearview mirror that the other vehicle was following us, Mr.S. informed me that we were staying in a hotel in Queens.

* * *

```
<Begin confession>

I had no clue what Queens was and where it was
located with respect to our office (which was in
Brooklyn.)

</End confession>
```

"Oh," I was terrified. "Why? I thought I was going to stay with you in an apartment."

"And you will," he nodded, "this is just temporary, for a couple of days, three tops. It's just that the apartment is already full right now. But the good news is that some programmers are heading back to India in a few days."

I nodded feebly. I was only thinking of the $400 I was carrying. If I had to stay in a hotel for a few days, the balance would be rapidly depleted, or even worse, I would be broke. I could end up with no money in a foreign land on my first day of work with no one to borrow from.

The taxi pulled in front of a hotel on Queens Boulevard.

```
<Begin confession>

I had no idea what a boulevard was. And for a
very long time after coming to America, I had
never seen it spelled fully. All the road signs
had the abbreviation of it. The green road sign
said Queens Blvd. I was only used to seeing the
road, street, *marg*, etc.

</End confession>
```
* * *

Obviously, the three of us stayed in one room. It made

economic sense. After all, all were thinking the same, *split the cost in three and stretch our dollars for a month.* The 29th of April was a Saturday. Yes, I left on the 29th and landed on the 29th after around twenty-four hours. How? The magic of time difference.

```
<Begin trivia>

When you fly from India to the US, you gain a
day, and when traveling from the US to India, you
lose a day. I know, rotation of our earth and all
the geeky astronomical stuff. I don't want to
bore you with that.

We have a time difference of around twelve hours
between LA and Mumbai. If you study the globe,
you'll see that Mumbai is literally on the other
side. Hence, when it's day here, it's night
there, and vice versa.

</End trivia>
```

After promising us that he would see us the next day (and take us to the Hindu temple), "If not for religious reasons, we can go there for the food. They have a wonderful cafeteria in the basement where they sell authentic South Indian food," he then looked at our hesitant faces, and added, "and it's cheap." Upon hearing cheap, my ears perked up. I could save some money.

"And believe me," he continued, "you will not realize it now, but soon you'll crave Indian food."

As promised, Mr.S. came and got us early the following morning. "We can reach there before they stop serving breakfast," he explained, "Our apartment is very close to the temple, so we can go there for a few hours and go back to the temple for lunch. While we are at the apartment, you can meet your colleagues."

"What about the programmers who were going to leave for India? Are they going tomorrow?" I asked.

"No," he shook his head, "I'm sorry, but they'll be gone by Monday." *This means one more day of a hotel stay,* I thought. He must have seen my crestfallen expressions. "Don't worry; I'll bring you to the apartment on Monday…no matter what."

I grinned. "Thank you."

We hailed a yellow taxi and sped towards our destination.

--*

When we reached the temple, as is the practice in the Hindu culture throughout India, we quickly took off our shoes and climbed the four steps which would lead us to the deity chamber. The familiar chants greeted us with a priest performing prayers. He held a shiny plate laden with lighted lamps in one hand while holding a small bell in the other. As he continued to chant, he would rotate the plate while jingling the bell. The familiar aroma of a lit incense stick wafted through the room. Several Indian families faced the deity with their hands folded in prayers and their eyes closed.

Soon, the prayers were over, and after bowing down and paying our respect to God, we hurried to the basement. We wanted to be there before they stopped serving breakfast. Fortunately, they were still open. We filled our bellies with a delicious breakfast of *medu-vada*[34], *sambar*[35], and coconut chutney.

We still were hungry. We ordered *upma*[36]. We ended our feast with a cup of steaming hot South Indian coffee.

---

[34] Medu vada is a South Indian breakfast snack made from *Vigna mungo* (black lentil). It is usually made in a doughnut shape, with a crispy exterior and soft interior. Source: Wikipedia.

[35] One of the versions of a sambar is a lentil-based vegetable stew, cooked with pigeon pea and tamarind broth. Source: Wikipedia.

[36] Upma, uppumavu, or uppittu is a dish originating from the Indian subcontinent, most common in Kerala, Andhra Pradesh, Tamil Nadu, Telangana, Karnataka, Maharashtrian, and Sri Lankan

After a satisfying breakfast, we walked to the apartment where Mr.S. was staying. It was a six-storied brick structure. Mr.S. led us to the staircases. "I'm on the second floor." When we were on the landing of the first floor, I was surprised to see Mr.S. walk toward the narrow corridor. I then remembered Mr.V. "The Indian second floor is equivalent to the first floor in the US." I followed him. Momentarily, he stood in front of the door with A201. He took out his key, unlocked it, and swung it open. "Come," he said. We gingerly entered. Four men greeted us. They were sitting on a square table in a corner and playing a card game. A few dollar bills were piled in the center, with some stacked in front of them. Four glasses were in front of them. *It has to be coffee, tea, or juice. It's way too early to have an alcoholic drink,* I thought.

Seeing us enter the room, they looked up, and Mr.S introduced us. They all nodded, waved, shook our hands, etc. (Honestly, I don't remember.) All I remember seeing is the scene of four Indians playing cards early in the morning. Mr.S showed us the apartment. It was a small apartment with one bedroom and a tiny kitchen. The living room consisted of two sofas that were perpendicular to one another. A small square, glass-covered table filled the space between them, and a lamp lay on top. A rectangular center-table lay in front of both the sofas. A few books on programming, data structures, and investment strategies were haphazardly strewn across

---

Tamil breakfast, cooked as a thick porridge from dry-roasted semolina or coarse rice flour.

the surface. An empty packet of cigarettes lay crumpled atop it. Mr.S. explained the sleeping arrangements. "There are five of us now. We are only allowed to have four. Two sleep on the sofa and the other two in the bedroom. The fifth person sleeps on the carpeted floor in a sleeping bag.

Which one of these is headed back to India, I wondered. They had completed their project and were headed back, and I was beginning my life in a new country.

Circle of life.

*_*_*

After overeating our lunch, we headed back to our hotel. We were to meet a lady, Pooja (name changed), in the evening who was working at DBC. She was going to take us out for dinner (*not too expensive,* I hoped.) Her apartment was very close (walking distance) to the hotel. We met her in our hotel's lobby (well, calling a tiny square a lobby is stretching it.) Pooja was a young girl in her twenties. She was thin and tall with straight hair and a pleasant face. A small *mangala sutra*[37] around her neck told us that she was married. She flashed a smile and proffered her hand. "Hi, I'm Pooja." We were slightly surprised as we were not used to shaking hands with women in India. We were used to folding our hands and doing a *namaste*[38].

---

[37] A mangala sutra is a necklace that the groom ties around the bride's neck in the Indian subcontinent, in a ceremony called Mangalya Dharanam (Sanskrit for '"wearing the auspicious"'). The necklace serves as a visual marker of status as a married Hindu woman. Source: Wikipedia.

"Hi," I shook her hand while nodding, and Rahul and Rajul did the same. She took us to a diner across the street (yes, I remembered to look in the opposite direction while crossing.)

```
<Begin confession>

I didn't know what a diner was. For a long time,
I thought that dinner was misspelled. I
attributed it to the American way of spelling
things. You know-check instead of cheque, tire
instead of tyre, curb instead of kerb, and so on.
In addition to these, I learned a whole new set
of vocabularies such as a walkway and not a
footpath, sidewalk instead of pavement, soccer
instead of football, and so many more. These are
all British words. To make things crazier, we use
some words in India that mean totally different
things here or are not used in America. Case in
point, okras. We call them lady fingers in India.
Or an eggplant. People in India refer to it as
brinjal. And the current cell phone generation
has derived a totally different meaning from an
eggplant emoji.

FOBs, do not, I repeat, do not, ask your ABCD
children what an eggplant emoji means. Just
google it.

</End confession>
```

Again, I digress. We entered the well-lit diner and

---

[38] Namaste, sometimes called namaskar and namaskaram, is a customary Hindu non-contact manner of respectfully greeting and honoring a person or group, used at any time of day. Source: Wikipedia.

found a table near a tall window that would allow us to look at the vehicles speeding by on Queens Blvd. A pleasant waitress brought us four shiny plastic menus with attractive photos of various dishes. My mouth began to water until my eyes fell upon the right-hand side of the dishes where the prices were written. I gulped as I mentally converted them into the Indian currency. Pooja was watching me with a knowing smirk. "It's my treat." I faked resistance but was relieved internally.

```
<Begin confession>
```

```
Over the years, I've noticed the same expression
on the faces of Indian people. The wheels are
churning in their brains as they convert the
price from dollars to rupees.
```

```
<Begin tip for Indian visitors coming from India>
Stop converting! Otherwise, you'll find
everything expensive. Life is too short. Enjoy.
</End tip for Indian visitors coming from India>
```

```
It has become a standard practice in most Indian
households to do a few things when someone visits
from India.
```

```
- Give them a sightseeing tour around LA (we call
it LA darshan.)
```

```
- Take them for a pilgrimage to Costco. They just
love that store. Which Indian can resist a
bargain price and large jumbo packs?
```

```
- Take them to the nearest beach (preferably one
with a pier as there are none in India.)
```

```
- Take them to Disneyland or Universal Studios
(depending on their preference.)
```

- Take them to The Cheesecake Factory or any
other restaurant to impress them. Obviously, they
never want to go to an Indian restaurant…duh.
These (or a variation of these) are a few things
every household does. However, as we spend more
time here, these things tend to get repetitive.
But I remind myself that these folks have minimal
time. I always suggest that they stick to one
coast and not try to cover the entire country.
After all, they have not come to put a checkbox
against the place visited.
Or have they?

</End confession>

After we ate, we stepped outside. It was dark already. We were so engrossed in picking up any tips Pooja had to give that we didn't even notice that we took over two hours at the diner. During our dinner, we had chivalrously offered to escort her to her apartment. However, we weren't so sure now. We had heard horror stories of people getting mugged. She saw the fear on our faces and offered to drop us at our hotel.

"We would have come, but it's dark now, and we fear that we might get lost," I said feebly.

"Of course, I totally get it," she gave us a knowing smile.

<Begin confession>

So, ladies and gentlemen, a lone woman in her
twenties escorted three men (who prided
themselves on being macho.) Till today, I think
of that comical scene that happened over thirty
years ago. It definitely deserves a spot in the

```
top-ten-terrified-moments.
```

```
</End confession>
```

We bade our goodnights and went up to our room. The following day was a Monday, the first day of work in a new country. As I lay in bed, waiting to fall asleep, I thought of my family and friends. I started to miss them until I fell asleep.

Chapter Eight

The following morning, we were dressed and ready when the phone rang. Mr.S. was waiting for us in the lobby. He took us to the subway station.

"To reach our office, we have to take two trains," he explained. He proceeded to teach us the ropes: where to buy a token (there wasn't a concept of purchasing a ticket,) how to use it to go through the steel barriers, the difference between uptown and downtown, etc. We were to take the 7 to 34th Street/Port Authority and change over to 2 or 3 to reach our final destination.

Basically, the city of New York is divided into five boroughs: Queens, Manhattan, Bronx, Brooklyn, and Staten Island. We were in Queens, and the DBC office was located in Brooklyn. We had to travel via Manhattan to reach our destination.

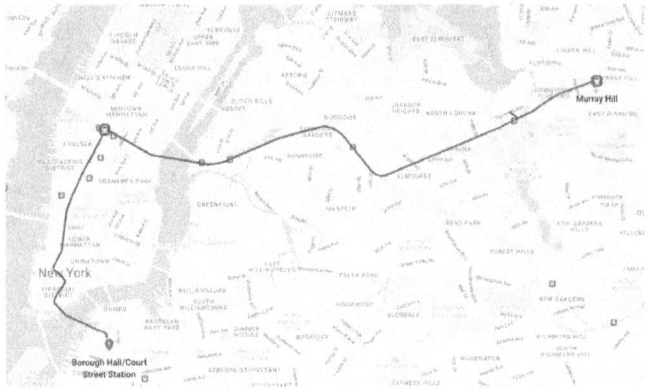

We looked at the map of the complex network of the subway system.

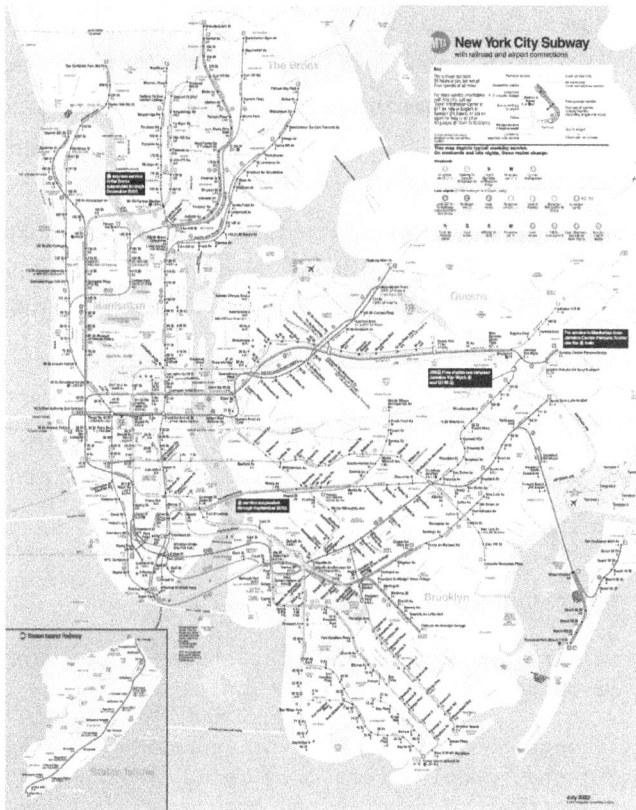

Being a proud Mumbaikar who had traveled daily by train, I must admit that I thought the Railway network we had was the most complex-until I saw this map.

When the train came, we pushed through the crowd (honestly, it is nothing compared to the trains in

Mumbai.) The announcer said "stand clear of the closing doors." Mr.S. warned us to stay away. Not being used to an enclosed compartment (the doors are always open in Mumbai trains. If they were shut, the sweltering humidity would suffocate the passengers.) It felt like tightly packed sardines in a steel tube. The train pushed off the station and made its way towards our destination. It was traveling high above the ground. Suddenly, without warning, we were engulfed by darkness.

34th street/Port Authority is one of the busiest stations in New York. It not only is a major junction for New York subways, but also is a hub for inter-state trains coming from the neighboring states.

```
<Begin trivia>
```

New York and the neighboring states of New Jersey and Connecticut make up the tri-state area.

Although the city of New York consists of five boroughs, people there only refer to Manhattan as 'the city.' To make things more confusing, New York City is just a tiny portion of the vast New York State.

New York City

Bronx

Manhattan

LaGuardia Airport

Queens

Newark Liberty
International Airport

Brooklyn

John F. Kennedy
International Airport

Staten Island

New York is a big state bordering Canada to its north, and New York City is at the southernmost tip. Several states border it on its eastern border.

</End Trivia>

We hurried to the next train that would take us under the East River to Borough Street station in Brooklyn Heights. Mr.S. smiled when he saw our wide-eyed, amazed faces. He must be thinking *been there, done that.*

<Begin confession>

```
Even after over three decades in this country, I
never get tired of seeing the awed expressions of
people who visit the US for the first time. The
look is priceless. I can relate to what must be
going through their minds.
```

* * *

```
</End confession>
```

We followed Mr.S. to the end of the platform, where the stairs led us to the street level. We exited the station and made our way to the DBC office.

Full of excitement and apprehension, not knowing what lay ahead. However, one thing was for sure—we were determined to succeed.

*_*_*

DBC's office building was a two-storied brick structure with tall windows. It's the very last building on the edge of the East River. Beyond the river is the famous skyline of Manhattan. We saw the world-famous Statue of Liberty to our left and the Twin Towers to our right. Adjacent to the building was a chain-linked parking area.

```
<Begin confession>

None of us (well, not none—only one) had a
vehicle. Even Mr.S didn't have one. Hence, the
parking lot was sparsely populated with cars of
Donn, the secretary, and the marketing team (who
were all Americans, whereas all the programmers
were Indians.)

<End confession>
```

A green door was in the middle of the building, followed by one more door. "It's meant to keep the cold out during winter," Mr.S. explained as he led us to the flight of stairs in the corner. On the second floor was a wooden door with a glass frame on top. Data Basics Corp. was etched in blue. Mr.S. swung it open. "Come." I inhaled deeply as I went in.

It was in a large room with high ceilings. In the center of the room were circular pillars at a regular interval. Four columns of gray desks went perpendicularly in the rectangle-shaped room. Each column consisted of ten desks. On one side of the large room were three smaller rooms, and on the far side was a door that led to the media room that housed circular tapes used in IBM computers. Next to it was a glassed room that had the Mainframes. Next to it was a blue partition, and behind it was the AS/400. Each desk had a bulky terminal. Each of them connected to either of the machines (the technology to have a single terminal to switch between the two machines didn't exist yet, or if it did, we didn't have it.)

On the room's left side was an entrance leading to the large kitchen. Mr.S. showed us around. "The corner room to our right is Donn's office; the receptionist sits in the middle room, followed by my room. Behind these rooms is an area where the marketing team sits." He led us into the kitchen. There was a long white table with twenty chairs around it. On the opposite side of the kitchen was a door. Mr.S pointed to it. "That leads to the restrooms; he then smiled. "By the way, that is the only room with a view of the Statue of Liberty, and that too is a partial view through the narrow windows. If you want a panoramic view of the Statue of Liberty and the Manhattan skyline, you have to go to the terrace." He pointed to the ceiling.

He led me to an empty desk. "You'll be sitting here. Get yourself familiarized." He walked towards his room after showing Rajul and Rahul their desks. I looked around at the empty desk. Apart from the tilted, bulky terminal, the only other item was a black ashtray. *Oh good, I can smoke,* I thought. My desk was on the opposite side of the kitchen. Sunlight seeped through the tall bay windows overlooking the street below. The multi-layered and heavily trafficked (a perpetual parking lot) Brooklyn-Queen Expressway lay above the road.

I looked around. Few desks were occupied by programmers busily typing on their keyboards. A lit cigarette dangled from the mouths of some. A few more programmers walked through the door and went to their respective desks as time passed. My face lit up when I saw the familiar face of Pooja. "Hi," I waved enthusiastically, and she acknowledged it with a smile before disappearing through the kitchen door.

Suddenly, there was a hushed silence as Donn walked through the door. He was casually dressed in blue pants and a white shirt. Upon seeing me, he smiled and waved. "Welcome." He was on the other end of the room. My desk was located on the opposite side of the room.

"Thank you," I mouthed.

After a few minutes, an African-American lady walked in. She was huge with a rounded face and puffy cheeks.

"That's the secretary," whispered a programmer behind me. I turned around. A young man in his twenties was smiling at me. He wore thick glasses. He wore a white shirt with blue squares. He smiled, proffering his hand. "Hi, I'm Sandy."

"Hi," I shook his hand. *Sandy?! A girl's name. Must have shortened it to 'Americanize' it,* I smiled to myself.

```
<Begin confession>

Many Indians have a 'restaurant name' for the
host or the hostess. They use it when making a
reservation. Many of us have a long and
complicated name for a non-Indian to pronounce.
Hence, they either shorten it or change it for
convenience.

Nowadays, it's more convenient to have a short
name. Imagine a barista trying to write a long,
multi-syllable name on a cup of coffee.
```

Soon, Donn called us into his office to assign our tasks. Rahul was to go to a client site while Rajul and I would be staying at the New York office. In addition, I was to assist Donn in demonstrating our software. DBC was IBM's Business Partner. One of the perks of being an IBM Business Partner was to use their offices all over the country. Typically, Donn and I would fly into a city where the potential customer was (located in the eastern half of the US) the previous day of the demonstration. I then would go to their offices and load the software (remember, the circular tapes? I might add, they were large and bulky. It was a challenge to carry them on an aircraft) on their mainframes or AS/400s (depending on what the client needed.) The following day the client (usually four to six people) arrived at IBM's premises. We would meet them at a 'demo room' and show them the software package. The whole demo would last around three hours.

<Begin confession>

Although I have been fortunate to visit many cities (thank you, Donn.) I've never stayed for more than two days. So, technically, have I visited several cities? Yes. Have I seen any of them (other than the IBM offices downtown?) No.

</End confession>

Chapter Nine

At the end of the day, Mr.S. came to take us back to our hotel. We were to go with him to his apartment. I was feeling relieved that I wouldn't have to spend one more day in the hotel. We had checked out in the morning and left our suitcases at the reception to avoid being charged for one more day's stay. During our subway ride back, Mr.S. was unusually quiet, not his chatty self. When we would ask him a question, he would reply in monosyllables. Finally, as we approached our hotel, we found out the reason behind his mysterious silence.

"There's a slight problem," he said.

We were alarmed. "What is it?" Rajul asked.

"It's not a big deal. You will have to adjust."

"Adjust?" my eyes narrowed. "To what?" I asked him suspiciously.

"Well," he looked at us sheepishly, "the programmers who were supposed to leave for India might have to stay for one more day."

"What?!" I almost shouted.

"I know," he shrugged matter-of-factly, "I'm sorry too, but hey, there's nothing I can do." I realized that his hands were tied too. As it is, he was accommodating three more people in his tiny apartment. "You know, it'll be an inconvenience for us too. But we all have to adjust."

I then realized what he meant. We all worked at the same office (which was a long commute), and even if we slept on the floor in a tiny apartment, it only had one bathroom to get ready.

```
<Begin confession>
```

Having lived in a one-bedroom flat in Mumbai with four (now five—my wife) of us staying in a small space, I was used to having many people live in a tiny area. However, we worked at different places that had different timings. So, we could stagger the use of one bathroom…as long as we finished our jobs in the bathroom before the water stopped.

Yes, we sometimes would have water cuts. Fortunately, it wasn't as severe as some other societies, where the water stopped at around 9 AM. Some folks may find it shocking, but it's a way of life in Mumbai.

Besides, some regions in the world are experiencing it too due to severe drought due to climate change. Yes, CLIMATE CHANGE IS REAL.

```
<Begin shameless plug>
```

As mentioned in my books in The Galaxy Series.

```
</End shameless plug>
```

```
</End confession>
```

"What do we do?" I asked him. He caressed his chin with a thoughtful look, but I could tell he had already thought of a solution. "Ah," he looked at us as if an idea had just struck him. "Here's what we do." He proceeded to narrate his solution. As he progressed, I realized what it meant. I balked at it but quickly realized that it was the most practical one.

"Okay," I reluctantly nodded. Both Rahul and Rajul agreed too.

"Great," Mr.S. clapped his hands cheerfully. "It's settled then. Now let's see. You all will need a sleeping bag tonight. Obviously, you don't have one."

We shook our heads. *How are we supposed to carry one from India?* I thought.

"Not to worry," he continued. "We have extra ones to spare. You can use them tonight."

--*

As we entered the apartment, we were greeted by the familiar aroma of an Indian curry. Having not eaten anything since lunch, my mouth began to water.

\<Begin confession\>

There was a small deli (a term I didn't know back then as we don't have the concept of a deli in India) across from our office that served fruits, salads, and sandwiches. It also served Chinese food, but Pooja warned me to avoid it.

"Sure, it looks very attractive, but our palates

are not used to the taste. So, don't waste your
money. And you'll be confused and overwhelmed by
the choices of sandwiches and salads. Besides,
many may have beef (a vast majority of Hindus
don't eat beef for religious reasons. Even after
so many years in this country, I enjoy the
confused look on the server of any fast food
establishment when I say, 'I'll have a hamburger,
but hold the burger.')"

I remembered her advice and stuck to fruits.

</End confession>

After having a rice and curry dinner, I plonked myself
on the sofa, lit a cigarette, and took a deep drag. As I
exhaled, Mr.S called me from the kitchen. "Come here." I
got up and walked into the kitchen: Mr.S. and a
programmer (who was cooking) were standing. I noticed
a faint twinkle of happy glee in the programmer's eyes.
"What is it?" I asked. Mr.S. pointed to the sink. "You
have to do the dishes." A pile-high of dishes, utensils, and
cooking pots were haphazardly stacked on one another.
Oh, no, I groaned as I remembered Mr.V.'s advice. *Learn to
cook; otherwise, you'll end up doing dishes.*

That night, lying in my sleeping bag on the carpeted
floor and looking at the rotating ceiling fan as Rajul
snored next to me, I ruminated on my first day and came
to one conclusion. I severely lacked in my skills—not in
programming, but in cooking. I had to rectify it quickly;
otherwise, I'd end up doing dishes for a long time.

*_*_*

* * *

I woke up at 4 AM the following morning. I rubbed my eyes and looked outside. It was dark. The street lights were still on. The city was still asleep. As decided, we would be getting up early to use the bathroom to get ready. We drew cards to determine who would go first. Unfortunately, I was the first one. I hurried to the bathroom to get ready. After shaving, I quickly jumped into the shower once I saw vapors emanating from the shower head. I dried myself and got into my office clothes. I saw the coffee machine in the corner as I passed the kitchen. However, I avoided the temptation of making a fresh brew. I knew that it would wake my nerves. *Not yet,* I thought as I headed back to the living room. I crouched down in my sleeping bag and gently whispered, "Hey, Rajul." He continued to snore. I repeated, "Rajul," a little louder this time, and patted him. "Wake up." He turned and slowly opened his eyes. "What time is it?"

"Half past four," I replied.

"Already?" he moaned as he turned his back to me, "Five more minutes."

"No," I turned him back. "You have to wake up now." He stretched himself lazily as he got up. I slid back into my sleeping bag (yes, fully dressed in the office attire) and went back to sleep.

Mr.S. had come up with this solution. The first person would wake up at 4 AM, use the bathroom, get ready, and then wake up the next person and get a few more hours of sleep. This relay would continue until the last person was ready. He then would wake, brew fresh coffee and wake up the rest. Since all of us would already be dressed to go, we would just have our coffees and head to the subway.

"Are all the others doing this too?" I asked Mr.S. when we were waiting for our train. "Yes, of course," he nodded. "Those who share an apartment do this; however, since there are three to four per apartment, the first person doesn't have to wake up so early. Besides, some prefer to live by themselves. In addition to this, one has to consider the travel time. Fortunately, we all are single."

"Well," I said, "not really. I know four of us are married: you, Rajul, Pooja, and I."

"Correct," he nodded, "however, all of us are single here."

"Oh, I see what you mean.," I shouted so that he could hear me over the thunderous noise of the train as it pulled into the platform. As I entered, I thought to myself, *I can't continue doing this.* I have to find something closer to the office. Otherwise, I'd end up waking up at ungodly hours. Even if the programmers left for India, at a minimum, four of us would be occupying it.

I decided to start looking for another apartment that very day. *Also, I have to learn how to cook very quickly,* I reminded myself.

Chapter Ten

When I walked into the office, I noticed a new face. He was busy hacking at his keyboard. I decided to go to his desk and introduce myself. He saw me approaching him and got up. He was wearing a gray suit and a loose blue tie around the collar of his white shirt. He was stockily built with a round face and bushy eyebrows. "Hi, I'm Sanjay," he smiled.

"Welcome," I shook his proffered hand. Having experienced it a day ago, I could relate to him on his first day on a job in a new country. However, my feeling of seniority was short-lived when I found out he had come to the US as a student a year ago. He graduated from the New Jersey Institute of Technology (NJIT).

```
<Begin confession>

He was the only programmer I knew who was brave
to reside in New Jersey and travel to Brooklyn.
Why brave? Remember, it was 1989. Mugging was
```

rampant. The Dotbusters[39] of New Jersey was a notorious gang.

</End confession>

Just then, Pooja joined us. I introduced her to Sanjay. "So, tell us, Pooja, what are you working on?" Each of us worked on different projects associated with different clients.

"Tits," she said.

My eyes widened. I looked at her in disbelief. Sanjay, too, was looking as if he had misheard her.

"E—excuse me," I stammered.

"Tits," she repeated nonchalantly. My jaw had dropped. I couldn't believe my ears.

"Tits?!" I mumbled.

"Yes," she nodded, "Tits. Toshiba Inventory Tracking System, TITS."

"Oh," I gave her a sheepish grin,

"TITS. What did you think?" It was apparent to both of us that the comedic irony of a ridiculous acronym was lost on her. She had been working on the project for a few months, taking the abbreviation for granted.

"Nothing," I replied, feeling guilty as I surreptitiously glanced at Sanjay. He, too, was grinning.

"Okay," she said. "I need to go back to my desk. Once she was gone, we burst out laughing. "Tits?" I laughed.

---

[39] The Dotbusters was a Hinduphobic hate group active in Jersey City, New Jersey from 1975 to 1993 that attacked and threatened South Asians, Source: Wikipedia.

"Tits? What kind of an acronym is that?"

"I know," Sanjay laughed, "I was thinking that it must be some sort of an exercise to enhance her boobs."

It would have been perfectly normal for Sanjay to assume that. Pooja wasn't well-endowed in her chest.

After chatting for a few more minutes, I went to my desk. The desk in front of me was empty. However, I realized it belonged to a programmer as several programming books were strewn on it. It also had an ashtray flowing with extinguished cigarette butts in gray ashes.

He must be running late, I thought to myself as I looked at my wristwatch. It was half past nine in the morning. I decided to call the secretary but noticed the instrument missing from my desk. I then looked around and noticed that none of the desks had them. I turned around to face Sandy (I still hadn't wrapped my brain around his name.) "Where are all the phones?"

"Oh, that," he exhaled. He then proceeded to explain that it was a recently implemented office policy. "If you want to make a phone call, you have to go to the receptionist's office," he said as I saw a fleeting smirk on his face. Was I imagining it? Later, I found out that I wasn't.

<Begin confession>

We were all terrified of the large (make that very large) African-American receptionist. Her overpowering physical attributes matched her piercing eyes and shrill voice, not to mention

```
her American accent that was hard to follow.

In fact, one of my good friends had given her a
nickname, Shurpanakha(a demoness in Hindu
mythology.)

</End confession>
```

Oblivious of this, I went to her office. "Excuse me."

"Yes?" she said, looking already annoyed that I was disturbing her morning ritual of hot coffee. "What do you want?" *She has already assumed that I'm here to use the telephone,* I thought.

"I want to search for an apartment," I replied, gulping my dry throat. "Can you guide me?"

"Oh," her demeanor softened when she realized I was not there to make a phone call. She reached for a newspaper that lay on her desk. "Here." I took it from her fat hands, "Thank you."

"Look at the classifieds. Narrow your search to Brooklyn. And then come to me. Brooklyn's a huge borough. Also, some parts of it are highly unsafe."

"Thank you so much," I smiled, "I really appreciate all your help."

Her eyes softened. A smile spread across her face. "You are welcome." She was enjoying her newfound position as a helper.

*_*_*

I went back to my desk and started to scan the classifieds. The desk in front of me was still unoccupied. I looked at my wristwatch again. It was nearing 10 AM. I turned around and asked Sandy. "Who sits here?"

"Oh," he looked up. "That's Kevin's (name changed) desk."

"Is he coming in today? I'd love to meet him."

"Oh," he said in a hushed voice, "you can't. In fact, he won't be in for a few months."

I was surprised. "Why?"

"He's in the hospital," he said softly.

"Oh, why?" I was concerned now. "Is he okay?" However, deep inside my mind, I knew it would be something more than a casual ailment for him to be out of commission for a few months.

Sandy looked at me with pained eyes. Or was it fear? "He was shot."

"*What?!*" my jaw dropped. I wasn't sure I had heard him right.

"He was shot," Sandy repeated. My entire body went numb. A chill ran through my spine as I was gripped with fear. *This is not happening. It's just a bad nightmare.* But it wasn't. For years, I had seen gun-toting Americans in Hollywood movies: soldiers, policemen, cowboys, the mafia, and many such characters. However, I never thought it could be a reality. Now it was hitting way too close for comfort.

"W—what happened?" I stammered, struggling to form a cohesive sentence.

Sandy took a deep breath. "Here's what I know so far. This happened just a few days ago, so stories are trickling

122

in."

"What is it?" I raised my voice. I wanted to know any little tidbits there were to hear. Having been only a few days in a new country and having heard horror stories of people getting mugged, my imagination was always in overdrive. And the news of the Central Park mugging was splashed all over the channels on TV. Sandy narrated the story.

Kevin had gone to a local bar after work. He was sitting on the bar counter and enjoying his beer. Just then, an off-duty police officer working for the transit system entered. He was barhopping and already intoxicated. He had been kicked out of the previous bar. However, he wanted more drinks. So, he came to this particular bar where Kevin was. He went to the counter and asked the bartender for a drink. Upon seeing that the cop was already drunk, the bartender refused. This enraged the cop. He whipped out his service gun and threatened the bartender. "Give me a drink, or I'll shoot you," he demanded. Upon seeing the weapon, the bartender got scared. He raised his hands and tried to pacify the cop. However, the cop was now enjoying his newfound power. He swung the gun at patrons and threatened them. He now was incoherently shouting while waving his gun. He started pointing the gun randomly. "Should I shoot you?" Unfortunately, Kevin happened to be sitting on a stool that was closest. The officer jabbed the barrel into his ribs. "Should I?" Kevin froze. Before he could react, the officer had pulled the trigger. The bullet pierced his left lung first and then his right lung and got lodged in his right arm (to this day, the bullet is still lodged in his upper arm. The surgeons have decided that it's safer if it stays there. I can't even begin to imagine what he has to go through now at the airports, having to explain to all the TSA officers when the metal detector goes off when they see an unknown object in his arm. Brown man carrying a suspicious thing on his person. Ergo, a terrorist.) He was rushed to the hospital, where he underwent several surgeries.

I was stunned. Blood had drained from my face. It looked as if I had seen a ghost just now. I didn't know what to say.

"We all are planning to visit him this evening," Sandy was saying, "would you like to join us?" However, I wasn't listening. Images of a bloodied person (I hadn't met Kevin yet, so I just imagined a random brown man.) danced across my face.

"Hello?" Sandy said, with a concerned look in his eyes, "are you okay?"

"Y—yes," I mumbled, "I think so."

"So, would you?"

"Would I what?"

"Would you like to join us?" he repeated as he realized I hadn't heard him. "We all are going to visit him at the hospital."

"Yes," I nodded feebly, "of course."

*_*_*

We have to find an apartment near our office soon," I told Rajul on our way back from the hospital. A dark cloud of gloom and doom hung over our imagination. "We can't afford to waste our time commuting. Besides, if the other programmers, who are leaving for India, have to stay longer, we will end up getting up at 4 AM till they leave."

"I agree," Rajul nodded. Rahul too agreed; however, he looked less concerned as he was assigned to travel to the client's site (Target) in Pennsylvania. He was leaving in a few days. He would be working there for four months before being reassigned to New Balance in Boston.

When we reached our apartment, I called Aruna *masi* (maternal aunt) in Brooklyn. She had been in the US for several years. She, along with her husband—Chandrakant *masa*, lived in Coney Island, Brooklyn. They had two children, a son, Paresh, and a daughter, Anjali. Paresh was a medical student studying to become a doctor and now he is a surgeon at NYU Hospital and their daughter is an executive at a leading bank.

```
<Begin confession>

Aruna masi is not my blood relative. She is my
mother's childhood neighbor's wife's sister. When
I met her, I wasn't even sure how I'd be
received. She was under no obligation to do much
for me (other than her obligatory duties of
inviting me for dinner.)

However, she has gone above and beyond. I'll
always be indebted to her and her family for
```

making me feel at home in a strange country.
There are innumerable occasions I can recollect
where she has been my guardian angel.

</End confession>

I was apprehensive about the call. I wasn't sure what to expect. "Hello," I said, introducing myself.

"Ah, yes yes," she said warmly, "my sister called me this morning. I was impressed that my *mami* (maternal uncle's wife) had called her from India.

<Begin confession>

Back then, phone calls to India were
prohibitively expensive. We hardly called home
and kept the conversation very brief. In addition
to this, the phone lines were pretty bad. One
could barely hear the person at the other end.
The person had to shout.
So, ABCDs, if you see your fobby relatives
raising their voice while talking to someone in
India, you now will know why.

I remember a guy we found working for the
telephone exchange in India. I used to call him
Pandit (I'm sure that is not his real name. Come
to think of it, I've never met him. A friend of
mine once told me a man would be calling me.
"Just give him the phone number you want to get
connected to," he said mysteriously.) Of course,
it all was very shady. However, I didn't care. I
just wanted to talk with my family for a long
time, so I didn't have to worry about the length
of the call (constantly looking at my
wristwatch.)

</End confession>

* * *

"Where are you staying?" She asked me.

"In Queens."

"And where is your workplace?"

"Brooklyn."

"*What?*" she was surprised. "That's far away."

"I know," I said. I then proceeded to tell her my sad story, ending with me wanting to find something closer. "I have identified several prospects but am unfamiliar with how close they are to my office."

"Ah," she exclaimed, "I can help you with that. I live in Brooklyn too."

"*Really?!*" I said, not realizing the rise of the decibel level in my voice. I gave her my office address.

"Oh, that's in Brooklyn Heights, and I'm at the other end of the borough—Coney Island."

"Oh, I see."

```
<Begin confession>

I had no clue where Coney Island was, how far it
was from Brooklyn Heights, or how to get there
from Queens. All I knew was that Aruna masi lived
in Brooklyn too.

</End confession>
```

I started to narrate the list of apartments I had circled. She quickly dismissed them all. They were either too far away, not in a safe neighborhood, or too expensive for me to afford (many of them didn't list the rent; however, she could identify the area they were in.)

My apartment search wasn't going well. I was crestfallen. I was silent for a while, desperate to find anything that would be more convenient than the current living arrangements.

"Tell you what," she finally said.

"What?"

"Why don't you come over to my house tomorrow for dinner? You can come straight from work. I'll try to look around for an apartment."

"That'll be great!" My mood lifted. "Thank you, *masi*. Oh, can I bring two of my friends? We all came together. They, too, are looking for an apartment."

"Sure."

--*

The following day after work, we took the F train to Sheepshead Bay Subway Station in Coney Island. Unlike the underground subway station of Borough Hall, the subway station was above the roads. When the doors slid open, we were greeted by the familiar smell of salty air that we had smelled in Mumbai (the city being on the coast of the Arabian Sea). We didn't know it then, but we were close to the world-famous Coney Island Boardwalk. We got off and climbed down to the street level. After a brisk walk, we reached our destination.

Aruna *masi*'s house was a multi-family two-story brick structure with a front driveway leading to a downstairs unit.

```
<Begin trivia>

These kinds of houses are mistakenly known as
mother-daughter houses.
A mother-daughter house is a single-family house
with two separate kitchens. Essentially, it has
two complete apartments, but it differs from
a multi-family home in that the apartments do not
have their own separate entrances. These kinds of
houses are common in Brooklyn, Queens, and Long
Island.

</End trivia>
```

Their house was on the second floor. A flight of stairs led to the front door. Hers was the corner house with rows of similar townhouses adjacent to one another.

We were greeted by the smiling face of young Anjali. The familiar aroma of Indian food being cooked wafted through the air. We then realized that we had not had a proper Indian meal since we left India. Suddenly, my craving for home food kicked in (I'm certain Rajul and Rahul felt the same.)

"Hi," she smiled pleasantly as she opened the door wider to welcome us, "come in. Mom's cooking in the kitchen. Mom, they are here."

Upon hearing this, Aruna *masi* came to greet us. "Come in," she smiled. We followed her to the living room. It was a rectangular room with a sofa that sat three. Next to it was a couch with a similar fabric with a floral pattern. On the opposite side was a large window that overlooked the street below. Chandrakant *masa* was reading a newspaper. Upon seeing us, he smiled and got up. "Welcome," he proffered his hand. We took it while introducing ourselves.

"Dinner will be ready in a few minutes. Paresh will be here any minute now. We can all eat together. After dinner, we can talk about your living arrangements."

"Did you find something?" I asked eagerly.

"Yes," she nodded.

```
<Begin confession>

Even if she had said no, our little trip would
not have been futile. Our bellies would be filled
with delicious Indian food.

</End confession>
```

* * *

Knowing she had lined up something for our sojourn, the food tasted more delicious. Soon, Paresh came. He was an affable young man with glasses and curly hair. We all ate together.

```
<Begin confession>

Three of us attacked the food as though we had
been starving for days. I'm sure all of them must
have had a good laugh about it after we left.
However, we didn't care. We didn't know when we
would get an authentic, home-cooked Indian meal
again.

<End confession>
```

After overstuffing ourselves, we sat in their living room.

"Can we talk about the apartment?" I immediately blurted out.

"I think so," Chandrakant *masa* nodded. "It might work for your needs."

"Where is it?"

"It's in Brooklyn, not very close to where you work. You'll have to go by subway. However, it's in a tranquil and safe neighborhood."

"Wonderful," I smiled enthusiastically. "We'd like to move in as soon as we can." *Tonight, if possible,* I was thinking. I was dreading having to get up at 4 AM.

"I'll talk to the landlord and see if you can move in tomorrow."

"That'll be great."

Chapter Eleven

The apartment (if you want to call it that) was in a Jewish neighborhood. Many ultra-orthodox Hasidic Jews live there. It was widespread to see them in their traditional garb of dark suit, white shirt, and a black hat with curly dreadlocks dangling on their temples (which rhythmically oscillated as they walked).

The house was a typical Brooklyn-style two-storied brick structure on the street lined with shaded trees. Vehicles were parked on both sides of the road. It was past noon. We were to meet the landlord. We looked at each other in excitement when we saw the house. "It looks very nice," I exclaimed. We hurried up the flight of five steps. We were now standing on the porch. Rahul rang the doorbell. "Coming," we heard a faint voice. We heard footsteps getting louder. The door swung open. A young man in a white tee and black trousers. He wore round glasses and had brown eyes. He wore a yamaka. The curly dreadlocks were short around his temple, showing his young age.

"Ah," he smiled as he stepped out on the porch and shook our hands, "you must be the ones here for the apartment. Mr. Shah called to inform me that you would be coming today."

"Yes," I nodded.

"But he informed me that you'll be coming this evening."

"Oh, I'm sorry," I apologized. "We decided to come early because we thought we could move in the evening. Is that going to be a problem?"

"No," he shook his head, "no problem. Come." He started towards the steps. We were surprised. We thought he would let us in the house to show us our apartment. "Follow me," he continued. He walked to the side of the house and unlatched the small iron gate that led to the side yard. In the middle of the sidewalls of the house was a brown door. He unlocked it, swung it open, and went through. We followed him. He flicked on a switch, and a white tube light flickered to life. We looked around. We were standing in a low-ceilinged kitchen. The floor was covered in shiny white linoleum. We could smell the strong odor of citrus. A refrigerator hummed in a corner next to the cream counters. An electric cooking range with four (various sized) coils was in the middle of the counter. On one side was a steel sink with a single faucet. I looked around. "This way," the landlord gestured, pointing at the refrigerator.

He disappeared behind it, and we gingerly followed him. "This is your bathroom," he pointed to a door. He proceeded to walk further, "and this is your room."

It was a tiny square room with freshly painted walls. It was large enough to fit three beds. It had no windows. A thick iron beam was in the middle, supporting the house above. The floor was covered in a thin green carpet (probably to cover the uneven dirt floor.)

We looked at each other, hiding our disappointment. *What do you say,* I raised my eyebrows. First, Rajul shook his head, and then he slowly nodded. I understood what he meant. *I don't like it, but it'll do.* Besides, we didn't have a choice. After all, beggars can't be choosers.

"Okay," I nodded, "we'll take it."

"Good," the landlord smiled. "I'll get the lease ready. When do you want to move? Oh, that's right, this evening. No problems. I'll be waiting with the paperwork for you to sign." He then frowned, "there's only one condition."

I looked at him suspiciously. "What?"

"Do not call me to fix anything on a Saturday."

I was confused. "Saturday? Why?"

"Sabbath."

"What is that?"

"It's a day of religious observance and abstinence from work, kept by Jewish people from Friday evening to Saturday evening." I later discovered he was a profoundly religious Jewish man who taught in a nearby synagogue.

"You can call me any other day if anything needs my attention," he continued. "I'll come and fix it."

As we were walking out of our basement apartment, I

noticed a large room on the other side of our apartment. It was dusty, dark, and cold, scattered with broken pieces of furniture. Cobwebs had formed in the corners. "It's an unfinished room. You are most welcome to use it too," he smiled when I asked him about it.

```
<Begin confession>
```

I now realize that although I was not happy with it, how lucky I was to stay there during warm temperatures. The basement apartment would have been damp and freezing during winter when it snowed in New York.

```
</End confession>
```

We moved in that evening. We knew that Rahul would be with us only for a short while. Rajul and I would be splitting the rent, making it affordable.

Fortunately, our landlord had provided us with a phone line. We made a quick call (under a minute) to inform our families that we had moved.

I went to the kitchen and opened the refrigerator. As expected, it was empty. I checked the cabinets above the counter, and again, empty. I slid open the cabinet drawers below the counter, thinking they too would be empty, but this time they were filled with various cutleries (and the most important thing, a beer bottle opener.)

```
<Begin confession>
```

There also was a corkscrew to open a wine bottle, but I wasn't a wine person.

* * *
</End confession>

I have to get some basic things for me to get started, I thought. The three of us walked to the nearest grocery store. As the doors slid open, we were in awe of what we saw. To describe the scene here doesn't do justice to it as most of us are now used to it. However, it was something behold in 1989—and that too coming from another country.

<Begin confession>

I grew up in a time when imports were strictly regulated in India. India was just a young country with little over forty years of independence. Unlike now, when travel abroad has become very common, I was fascinated with 'imported stuff' - may it be a perfume, a pair of jeans, a slice of cheese, or a box of chocolate. Anything 'imported' held a special place.

</End confession>

It was already dark when we returned, holding plastic bags filled with groceries. I busied myself in the kitchen, boiling potatoes. We were making potato curry.

*_*_*

I spent the next few days getting familiarized with how things worked in the US, not just work but life in general.

When people say it's a culture shock, I feel the word is an overused cliche but wholly justified. I not only had to worry about performing at work, but also had to get used to day-to-day living, from the simple task of getting a coffee to complex tasks like cooking. I could hear Mr.V.'s words of wisdom, "programming is the easiest part of being there." How right he was.

IBM's offices were located in Manhattan (the city). Whenever we had to demonstrate the software to a client, I would go there the previous day (with my circular and bulky tapes) to install the software. I remember when I went there the first time. I was awed by the highrises surrounding me and people in their fine attire of business suits and formal dresses going about at a brisk pace. After using the IBM data center to install the software, I headed back to the office. I had plenty of time before lunch, so I decided to get coffee. I stepped into a deli and went to the counter. Behind the counter, a fat man was busy attending to other customers. When it was my turn, he looked at my empty hands, "Yes?"

"A coffee, please."

"Oh." He turned around and slid an empty Styrofoam cup. I looked at him with a puzzled expression; however, I didn't want to expose myself as an FOB. Despite all my efforts to try hard to 'fit in,' he must have realized that I was new to this country.

<Begin confession>

No matter how hard we try, FOBs are easily

identifiable. Even after having been in the country for over three decades, I can easily be sniffed out as one. Sure, we dress differently now, drive expensive cars, have a different haircut, Americanize our accents, etc., but my children can easily tell the difference.

However, I must say that over the years, our population has grown and spread. The outcome of it is that we really don't care.

```
</End confession>
```

He pointed at a corner. There were two tall thermoses with a spout on top. Next to them was a tray filled with several cups. Each one of them was filled with different colored paper sachets. Next to them was a glass container filled with sugar. And finally, a tiny steel kettle.

Not knowing what to do, I walked across and stood next to it, all the while pretending I was perusing the shelf in front of me, trying to decide what to get. Just then, a beautiful lady with an empty cup came to the counter. From the corner of my eyes, I started to observe her surreptitiously.

She pumped the thermos lid several times until hot coffee sputtered from the nozzle. When her cup was almost full, she reached for the sugar glass container and tilted it. She then moved down the assembly line and poured milk from the kettle. Next, she reached for a flat wooden stirrer and started mixing the ingredients. She took a small sip to ensure she didn't need more sugar, milk, or coffee. When satisfied, she tossed the wooden stick in the trashcan next to the coffee station. She then covered the cup with a plastic lid to keep the liquid warm and exited the deli. The entire process must have taken less than sixty seconds to complete. I was highly impressed with her efficiency. Feeling confident, I approached the station and made a fresh cup of coffee.

Now, you must be thinking why I'm boring you with minute details of a simple task of making coffee. Let me explain. Back in Mumbai, when I ordered a cup of coffee, the cup was served to me with all the ingredients mixed. All I had to do was to bring it to my lips and savor a freshly brewed cup of coffee. In the U.S. on the other hand, one does everything on their own. DIY.

```
<Begin confession>
```

Due to the overabundance of highly cheap labor in India, FOBs are used to being served. Hence, they find it very challenging when they have to do things on their own in many Western countries.

When I was growing up, although we had a small one-bedroom flat, we would have three helpers to serve us. Yes, three. One to cook, one to do the dishes, and one to clean the house. To add to our laziness, we had a dhobi (a washerman or washerwoman) who washed and ironed our clothes. And now, if we need to buy anything from the grocery store, we just called the store owner, and he would deliver it (no minimum items or minimum price.) These are just a few examples; there are way too many to list here. Maybe that's one of the reasons FOBs find life more convenient there. It's a month-long vacation from not having to do daily chores such as vacuuming, doing the dishes, running to grocery stores, cooking, etc. (Of course, I'm only kidding. There are more than these mundane things that attract us to India.)

I admit that I was one of them; however, I've learned to be independent over the years, and now I really enjoy it. So much so that when I visit India, I hesitate to order around.

</End confession>

*_*_*

One evening, when I was busy in the kitchen, Rajul called me (Rahul had already left for Pennsylvania.)

"Call for you," he yelled from the other room.

I turned the knob to lower the heat intensity, wiped my hand on the kitchen towel, and went to the room to find Rajul holding the receiver. "It's your wife."

My heart leaped. I smiled. "Hello."

"Hi," I heard the melodious voice that never failed to put a silly grin on my face. "How are you?"

"I'm doing fine," I lied. I didn't want to break the dam of emotions I was desperately trying to hold. I could hear the faint sound of pitter-patter. "Is it raining already?"

"Yes, the monsoon came early this year." That made me more nostalgic for things we used to do in the rains (again, way too many to list. If you have grown up in India, close your eyes for a moment to enjoy the reverie of your fond monsoon moments. India is a vast country, and Mumbai is just one city. You might experience a different moment in another town; however, I'm sure the underlying feeling is quite similar.) After our own '*Pandit*,' we would talk more frequently and for a more extended period (without having to keep an eye on the clock.) However, she sounded different this time. I couldn't detect what it was. *Nervousness? Joy? Apprehension? Worry?* I thought. "What is it?" I said aloud.

"I'm pregnant," she blurted.

"*What?!*" I screamed. My heart skipped a few beats, my face contorted, oscillating from a silly grin to a concerned look. Within a split second, I transformed from a married man to a father. It's difficult to describe the emotional rollercoaster I went through within a span of a few seconds. Only those who have experienced it can relate to it.

I now understood the change in her tone. "Wow!" I said.

```
<Begin confession>

Honestly, I don't remember what I said or how I
reacted. However, one thing's for sure - I must
have sounded goofy.

</End confession>
```

"T—that's wonderful news!" I continued to stammer. I don't remember how long or what else we talked about. All I remember is that it was more than a minute (thank you, *Pandit*). When I hung up, I looked at Rajul and smiled. "I'm going to be a father."

"Congratulations, man," he gave me a big hug. "This calls for a celebration." He went to the kitchen and returned two cans of chilled beer. He handed one to me and opened his; I did the same. "Cheers," we touched the cans briefly before taking a large gulp. We sat on our spring beds across from each other. His expression turned serious, and his tone lowered, "You know what this means, right?"

"What?"

"Either you must go back, or she has to come here."

"I can't go back so soon. I don't have enough money to fly back. Besides, Mafatlal will sue me. Remember, we signed a six-month contract."

"That's right," he nodded. "I forgot about it."

"Besides, let's assume that Mafatlal doesn't take any legal actions. Even then, the least they'll do for sure is to let me go. So, I'll be an unemployed father-to-be."

```
<Begin confession>

I didn't tell Rajul that I feared being labeled a
loser among my friends and relatives.

</End confession>
```

Suddenly, the happy atmosphere of celebration turned into a cloud of gloom. We both took a few more gulps, lost in our own thoughts.

"What do I do?" I finally said.

"Well," Rajul looked at me with finality, "you really have one choice now."

"What is that?"

"She has to come here."

*_*_*

I called my wife the same evening and told her about what Rajul and I had discussed. "You have to come," I reiterated.

"B—but," she sounded doubtful.

"But, what?"

"I will have to resign from my job." She had taken up a professor position at an arts college (professor sounds pretentious for a woman in her twenties.)

"Then do it."

"I still have to get a visa," she continued.

"Don't you have one?" I asked, "you were already here as a tourist." My wife had come to the US as a visitor in 1986.

"That has expired."

"Oh," I said, "apply for a new one then. I'm sure it'll be much easier to get one the second time."

"I think so," she said. I could tell that she was slowly psyching herself to come here.

```
<Begin confession>
```

```
I can't even begin to imagine what must have been
going through her mind. In India, a woman leaves
her own family to join her husband's family. That
in itself is highly emotional. To be with
strangers. The only person you know is your
husband. Even if you had a love marriage.
However, a vast majority of marriages in India
```

```
are arranged. Thus, the groom, too, is a
stranger.

Fortunately, we had a love marriage. We dated for
five years before we got married. Hence, she knew
me well.
However, leaving her family to spend life with me
was emotional in itself. Now I'm asking her to do
it once again. And this time there would be more
stress of being pregnant, leaving everyone she
knew behind, and moving to an unknown country.

My hats off to her and all the women who have
gone through this.

</End confession>
```

"Okay," she finally said.

"Yay! I pumped my fist. We talked for a little longer to thrash out the details and the logistics of coming here.

*_*_*

She called me in a few days to inform me that she had been granted the visa. I couldn't conceal my relief. Having heard many stories of people getting rejected at the US Consulate, I knew how difficult it was to obtain one.

"I want to celebrate my birthday with you," she said.

"Huh," I was pleasantly surprised. "That's less than a month away."

"Yes," she said matter-of-factly. *Of course, she knows her own birthday,* I thought.

"Okay."

When I disconnected, it dawned on me that I had to start looking for a separate apartment (just for the two of us). I couldn't have her living in a basement. It worried me as I was the only programmer at DBC that would be living with a wife. Either most of them were single, or they had their spouses in India. That meant I would be absorbing the entire rent—no more sharing-the-rent business. I had to find something within my budget (remember, I got $1,000 of monthly living expenses) in a safe neighborhood and near the office—that narrowed my options down to Brooklyn.

Suddenly, the American dream seemed like an American nightmare.

Chapter Twelve

A year before my arrival, my college friend from Mithibai, Subra, had come to the US for his Master's. He was a massively built man with broad shoulders. Like most Indian men, he, too, sported a thick mustache. He had a gregarious personality. When he laughed, his entire body shook. It was infectious.

Subra was one of the most intelligent people I've met. Back in our college days, when we were busy studying at the library, I always saw him helping someone solve a problem. He was naturally gifted with a sharp memory. I had never seen him with his nose buried in a book. I always wondered when he studied.

Upon seeing me, he lifted me in a bear hug in his giant arms.

"So good to see you," he exclaimed as he put me down.

```
<Begin confession>

I found it very strange (and embarrassing) to see
a grown man hug so tightly. We Indian men are not
```

supposed to display our emotions overtly.
Remember the British motto? Keep Calm and Carry
On, keep a stiff upper lip, etc. Moreover, I
don't remember ever hugging him back in my
college days.

</End confession>

"Come in, let me show you my apartment," I said as I guided him. He looked around, surveying the kitchen as we passed it to our room. We sat across from each other on the bed.

"Would you like some beer?" I asked.

"Sure," he nodded.

I went to the kitchen, opened the refrigerator, and reached for two chilled cans. I returned with them and gave him one. "Here."

"Thanks," he said as he opened it and held his arm high. "Cheers."

I reciprocated, and we took a large swig. After a few minutes of silence—while we enjoyed the chilled brew—we reminisced about our Canteen days.

"Is anyone else from our college here?" I asked.

"Not that I know of," he shook his head, "but I'm sure there are quite a few ex-Mithibai students spread across the country."

"How are you doing at the university?"

"I'm doing fine," he shrugged. "Getting adjusted to campus life."

He was a student at Rensselaer Polytechnic Institute (RPI), located in the city of Troy in upstate New York—near the capital city of Albany. He came to visit me over the weekend. Boy, was I glad to see a familiar face?!

I wanted to know more about his life in a new country. I asked him many questions, which he answered patiently. He then asked me how I was adjusting.

That's when I informed him about my dilemma. On the one hand, I was happy to share the news of me becoming a father; on the other hand, I expressed my concerns about finding an affordable apartment. Being a student with a limited budget, he could relate to my story.

```
<Begin confession>
```

```
In addition, we know each other from our Canteen
days when we were perpetually broke. We have
shared a cigarette, a snack, a drink, or a small
glass of tea (aka cutting tea) where we asked our
server to do a 'one-by-two.' Folks here may
wonder what 'one-by-two' is, but I'm sure many
get it. Hence, if there was anyone in the US who
could understand where I was coming from, it was
Subra.
```

```
</End confession>
```

He remained silent for a while. I could see his mental wheels churning. He finally smiled.

He took a large swig and looked at me. "Don't worry. I think I can help you with that."

"How?" I asked suspiciously. I was moved by his good intentions but was unsure if he could do anything to alleviate my situation. Subra was a dependable friend in times of need.

However, it so happened that he actually could help

me. He informed me that he had a fellow student, Bill, who had an apartment in Brooklyn. It was a small studio apartment that had been converted into a one-bedroom. It wasn't far from where I was currently staying. The other advantage was that it was on the first (Indian ground) floor.

It would be highly convenient for a pregnant wife, I thought.

It sounded perfect; however, I didn't want to raise my hopes. "What's the rent?"

"I don't know," Subra shrugged his shoulders. "I can find out from Bill. Can I make a call?"

"Sure," I pointed to the phone.

He dialed Bill's number (which he knew by heart. Of course, razor-sharp memory) and spoke to him briefly. After disconnecting, he took a deep breath as he looked at me. "$450."

```
<Begin confession>

$450 nowadays sounds like a bargain. However,
this was in 1989. Ask anyone you know who came in
1989 with almost no money. I'm sure they have a
sob story to narrate.

</End confession>
```

Upon hearing the amount, I was a little disappointed. Almost half of my monthly allowance would be spent on rent. It was within my range, but I'd have to budget my other expenses tightly. The two of us (soon to be three) would have to live on $550 for the rest of the month.

* * *

```
<Begin confession>

I had not even figured out the initial cost of
settling in a new apartment. I would have to end
up spending on buying cookware, cutleries,
kitchen supplies, bathroom supplies, and so on.
There were way too many things I had not thought
of.

This is where Aruna masi came to my rescue. She
helped me settle in. She gave me so many things.
She also gave me a small television besides the
essential pots and pans for cooking. She was my
guardian angel.

Fortunately, the apartment was furnished with a
bed, a sofa, a small cot, a small dining room,
and a center table.

</End confession>
```

Subra looked at me intently. "What are you thinking?"

"I'm just calculating my expenses to determine if I can afford it."

"If I were you, I'd go for it. Trust me. You won't get a better price."

We stayed silent for a while. I was doing mental math, and he patiently awaited my decision.

"Okay," I finally said. "I'll take it."

"Great," Subra raised his beer can. "I'll tell Bill."

Chapter Thirteen

In a few days, Bill mailed me the keys and the address to the apartment. It wasn't very far from our current apartment—probably around fifteen minutes of walk. I decided to check out the apartment; however, I wasn't ready to move in.

```
<Begin confession>

I was scared of living alone. My imagination was
running amuck. Images of a bleeding Kevin danced
across my face. The recent incident of the
Central Park attacks also didn't help.

</End confession>
```

When I returned from work, I asked Rajul to come with me. The sun had disappeared behind the buildings. It was twilight but getting dark. The street lights mounted atop the tall lamp posts cast a circular halo on the sidewalk. A cool breeze was gently caressing our faces. A few pedestrians were passing by. I turned my head to glance at the boulevard casually. The headlights of the passing by vehicles had been turned on.

<Begin confession>

Unlike in India, vehicles hardly ever honk. The noise pollution in India will hit anyone who travels there for the first time. Here, a car horn is very sparingly used: to draw someone's attention, to express annoyance, or to insult. Whereas in India, it's constantly used to communicate, not only with the traffic, but also with the pedestrians—as if to warn them: watch out, there's a vehicle behind you.

</End confession>

Both of us had our hands in our pockets and were walking with our heads down, all the while surreptitiously scanning our surroundings, ready to spring into a sprint at the slightest threat.

<Begin confession>

Unlike the brave karate man in India, I was nervous about getting mugged. To heighten my fears, I had heard of a few horror stories from people recently returning from the U.S. when I was in India.

"You don't know what kind of weapon the opposite person is carrying. If you are lucky, he may only have a knife on him. You can easily run away. However, running won't help you alone if he has a gun. You must run in a zig-zag pattern, keep ducking, and hope that your attacker misses."

* * *

And how is this supposed to help me? I wondered.
</End confession>

"Hey," I casually asked.

"Yes?"

"Do you have $1 bills?"

"I think so. Why?"

"Can you give me five $1 bills? I'll return them to you as soon as we return to our apartment."

"Of course," he nodded, "but why?" It was a bizarre request.

"Just hand them over to me; I'll explain it to you later," I held out my hand. Rajul put five $1 bills in my palm. I then proceeded to distribute them in different pockets— my shirt and my trousers. Rajul narrowed his eyes, witnessing this strange and mysterious behavior.

"What are you doing?" he asked.

Ignoring him, I continued to distribute the $1 bills. Thankfully, he didn't pursue the matter any further.

Soon, we reached the apartment and quickly surveyed it. I was cognizant of the fact that it would be getting dark soon.

We walked through the small apartment. Everything seemed to be tidy. I went to the tiny kitchen and opened the drawers. They were stocked with utensils. A small refrigerator hummed quietly on one side. I opened it. It was empty.

"Looks good to me," he said. He had opened the main door to the apartment and was standing with one foot inside the apartment and the other outside, indicating that he was ready to go.

"Me too," I agreed.

"Let's go," he cocked his head.

"Okay," I nodded as we walked out of the apartment, shut the door behind us, and locked it.

Just then, a burly man walked past us. He looked at us curiously as he opened the door next to us.

He must be my new neighbor, I thought. I contemplated introducing myself but decided against it as it was getting dark.

"Let's go," Rajul said again when he saw that I had stopped.

"Okay," I nodded as I followed him.

When we stepped out of the apartment building, it was already dark. Nervously, we picked up the pace while returning to our basement apartment.

When we returned to the basement 'dungeon' (as I called it), we felt a sense of being safe and secure.

I handed him the $1 bills. "Thank you."

"Sure," he shrugged as he shoved them in his pocket. "What was that all about?"

I didn't reply, ignoring his question.

"What was that all about?" he repeated, louder this time. I looked at him sheepishly, "promise me you won't make fun of me."

"What? Why?" he looked confused.

"First, promise me."

"Okay, I promise."

"For protection." I averted his eyes.

"From what?"

"Mugging?" I mumbled as I continued to look down.

"Huh? Mugging? What do you mean?" his confusion deepened.

I didn't reply immediately. However, I realized there was no escaping from it now. Besides, in my heart, I knew that if there were one person who could relate to how I felt, it would be Rajul. I, however, dreaded all the teasing that would ensue once he told Rahul (hence the promise).

"W—well," I finally confessed, "I took the money from you in case I got mugged, and someone demanded to hand over the cash."

"Oh," Rajul concealed his smirk, "but why distribute it in different pockets?"

"In case I got mugged again," I grinned sheepishly, averting his eyes.

Soon, we busied ourselves in the kitchen. It was my turn to cook (and Rajul's to be my victim.) In a little while, the aroma of Indian food wafted throughout the tiny apartment.

When it was ready, we filled our plates with a mound of white rice and topped it off with a generous helping of *daal* and a spoonful of mango pickle on the side. As Rajul mixed the rice and *daal* and took the first bite, he scrunched his face.

"What's wrong? Too hot?" I asked him.

"N—no," he coughed. "Next time, use less *rai* (mustard seeds)."

Poor Rajul.

* * *

I was counting the days as I eagerly awaited my wife's arrival. I took a subway to reach JFK Airport. Thankfully, her flight was landing in the afternoon. I took a half day off from my work. I took a subway and changed to Airtrain to reach JFK airport. My excitement rose as I stepped into the vast terminal for international arrivals. I could hardly wipe off the perpetual silly grin plastered across my face.

JFK Airport was teeming with activity. Hundreds of people were eagerly awaiting the arrival of their loved ones. Many were carrying heart-shaped balloons, boxes of fancy chocolates, and flower bouquets. *I should have gotten one,* I cursed myself. I saw a flower shop on one side and considered getting one but decided against it (yes, a limited budget prohibits one from being too indulgent and romantic.) The passengers would come through wide doors after clearing their customs inspection. When they spotted their loved ones, their faces would light up. They would hurriedly wheel their suitcases-laden carts and greet them with a big hug.

```
<Begin personal observation>
```

JFK Airport sums up the true melting pot America is. You will witness different colored people with various features, speaking a foreign language and different garb. However, one thing is common. They all have a dream to succeed in the Land of Promise - no matter what the year may be. It can be 1889, 1989, or 2022. All they want is happiness and freedom.

* * *

```
</End personal observation>
```

I smiled to myself as I remembered the same scene several days ago when I walked through the arrival doors. I craned my neck and lifted my toes to get a view over the crowds of heads.

Finally, I saw her. She was gingerly walking as she scanned the crowd, looking for a familiar face. She wore a traditional Indian attire of white *Salwar Kameez*[40] with a green paisley pattern and an orange *dupatta*[41]. She looked lost and nervous. She steered her cart slowly as she continued to look for me.

"Here," I waved enthusiastically. However, she continued to scan the crowd. "*Hey, here!*" I waved with my hands, jumping up and down. She looked in my direction for a brief moment, then looked past me and continued looking for me. She turned around to see who I was waving at. It was apparent that she did not recognize me.

"*Hello,*" I waved again, a little perplexed this time. *Why doesn't she recognize me?* This time, she looked at me. Her eyes narrowed. "It's me," I smiled as I waved again. Her

---

[40] Salwar Kameez is a traditional combination dress worn by women, and in some regions by men, in South Asia. Source: Wikipedia.

[41] The dupatta is a shawl traditionally worn by women in Indian subcontinent to cover the head and shoulders. The dupatta is currently used most commonly as part of the women's shalwar kameez outfit. Source: Wikipedia.

face fell. What was wrong with her? That wasn't the reaction I expected (I was expecting a big smile and a tight embrace.)

She strolled towards me. Her expression turned more into shock. "What have you done?"

I was confused. *What have I done?* I thought as I stood there with my arms open. Then it struck me.

Of course.

```
<Begin confession>

When I was in Mumbai, I always had a mustache.
However, the day I landed here, I shaved it off.
I figured that it was a fresh start with a new
look. The only people who had seen me sporting a
mustache were Rahul and Rajul (and Donn). The
others would see me for the first time, so they
would assume that that's how I always looked. I
then would grow it back upon my return. After a
day or two, I had gotten used to my new looks.

However, I had not anticipated these sudden turns
of events. I was now standing in front of a woman
who didn't recognize her own husband.

</End confession>
```

"Oh, this?" I smiled as I placed my index finger on my upper lip.

"Yes," she nodded. Her eyes moved down my face. "*That!*" she glared, showing her displeasure.

"It's nothing," I shrugged casually. "I just wanted a new look." I opened my arms. "Now, can I get a hug?" However, she was too taken aback to adjust to my new look mentally. *I should give her some time*, I thought.

"But I liked your old look," she complained.

"Don't worry," I said as I wrapped my palms around the cart's handlebars. "You'll get used to it."

"And if I don't?" she asked as she let me commandeer the cart.

"I'll grow it back then," I smiled.

"Promise?"

"Promise," I replied as we headed towards the exit. We hailed a yellow taxi and gave the driver Aruna *masi's* address.

On our way to her house, I tightly held her hand as I wondered what must be going through her mind.

```
<Begin confession>

I now realize how stressful it must have been for
a pregnant woman to travel for an extended period
and meet her husband, who looked totally
different from the man she had fallen in love
with.

<End confession>
```

We chatted excitedly, me wanting to know about her life in India, and her wanting to know about mine in the US. I was just happy to see her.

"How's everyone in India?" I asked.

"Good," she replied. "How're you doing here?"

"Okay...I guess," I shrugged.

"You guess?"

I looked at her and smiled. "Yes, it's hard living like a

bachelor. You are the first spouse to come over here. The rest all live here as bachelors. Many of them have already started to drop subtle hints of their desire to come over for dinner."

"And what did you tell them?"

"I told them about you being pregnant."

"Good," she smiled.

I had already told her about our apartment over the phone. "I can't wait for you to get here so we can move in together."

"Me too," she said, "you know I'm coming early so I can spend my birthday with you, right?"

"Yes," I nodded, remembering our conversation. Her family wanted her to stay back in India for a few more days so that they could celebrate her birthday. However, she had insisted on coming here to celebrate it with me.

I felt special, and I wanted to make it a special day for her—a day she would remember for the rest of her life.

Chapter Fourteen

We moved to our new apartment, eagerly trying to make out lives in a new country. We had started with the essential utilities, but didn't have a phone connection yet. It would be a few days before we got one.

```
<Begin confession>
```

```
Another wondrous thing. Having come from a
country where one had to wait years to get a
phone connection, getting one in just a few days
was unheard of.
```

```
</End confession>
```

```
<Begin confession>
```

```
When my wife was packing to come to the US, she
didn't pack any masalas to make Indian meals as I
had come here less than a month ago. My mother
had packed a year's supply. Upon her arrival, my
wife was shocked to find out that I had exhausted
them in less than a month. "What did you do?" she
laughed (and still made fun of me).
Poor Rajul, who had to endure my atrocious
culinary skills. Sorry, my friend.
```

My apartment was a brief walk to the subway station (Cortelyou Road). After having morning coffee, I would head there holding a brown briefcase.

Upon reaching the office, I was informed by our marketing guy, Dave, that he had to fly for a client meeting the next day and he needed a program to be ready before that. I immediately got busy writing and debugging the program. I didn't realize it was getting late. Suddenly, I looked up from my screen and looked out the windows. It was dark—way past my usual office hours. There was no way I was taking the subway so late. I expressed my concerns to Dave, and he assured me I would be compensated for my taxi fare.

There was one problem. I hadn't informed my wife. There was no means of reaching her. I didn't even know my neighbor, so I could call him to relay the message. She was expecting me to be back by six or six-thirty (at the latest by seven). As time progressed, the evening turned into night. There was no way for a pregnant lady to venture out into an unknown country. Besides, where would she go? She didn't know my workplace or where Aruna *masi* lived. She had no choice but to turn to one person.

God.

She started to pray. Finally, in the middle of the night, I reached the apartment. I'll never forget the scene I saw when I unlocked the door. My wife is on the bed with puffy eyes, surrounded by deities of different Gods. Her eyes were shut tight as her lips moved, praying to the Gods. Upon hearing me enter, she opened her eyes, burst into tears, shook her head, and ran to me. I hugged her tightly. "Hey, It's okay. I'm fine."

She pounded her fist on my chest as she buried her head in my shoulders. *"What's wrong with you?"* she screamed. I had no defense. Even when I narrate this story now, I can see her eyes narrowing in anger.

```
<Begin confession>
```

```
How insensitive of me to find humor in a
traumatic experience. Anything could have
happened that night. ANYTHING. She could have
miscarried our daughter.
```

```
She flew early to ensure that she celebrated her
birthday with me. And in return, I made it into
the most traumatic day in her life.
Sorry, dear.
```

```
</End confession>
```

* * *

*_*_*

As days turned into weeks and weeks into months, my wife's belly was growing. Cold season swooped in when the weather changed, the trees started to shed their leaves, and the days got shorter.

I distinctly remember my first snow. Coming from Mumbai, I had never seen it in my life. We merely have three kinds of weather: winter (extremely mild), summer (extremely hot and humid), and monsoon (very heavy rains). When I saw the white powder falling from the sky, I ran out in my shorts (the apartment had central heating.) After a little while, I ran back in when I started to shiver.

My wife would go to Coney Island Hospital for her prenatal checkup. The problem was that we didn't have any insurance; hence she had to go to the general ward. Fortunately, both Aruna *masi* and Chandrakant *masa* worked there. He was a lab technician, and she was a data-entry operator. She showed my wife the ropes. On many occasions, my wife would go in the morning, and her turn would come late in the afternoon. She could not do anything but await her turn without proper nourishments. Fortunately, Aruna *masi* lived nearby. She would take her to her house, feed her lunch, and drop her at our apartment. That was a major relief as I was always worried about my wife having to endure the slippery road conditions to take a bus to reach the hospital.

Moreover, their son, Paresh (who is a successful surgeon now), was attending medical college. He would volunteer to come over and do a quick checkup with my wife to see how her pregnancy was progressing.

These all were gestures that are imprinted in my memory. After all, we were living on a tight budget of $550 a month. We would literally calculate (to the dollar) the amount we could afford to spend: Subway tokens and groceries (milk, vegetables, etc.). No more money was left to enjoy life, go to the city (Manhattan), and so on.

One of the things I missed the most was cricket (did I tell you I'm a big cricket fan?) Unlike today, we didn't have any means to (that I knew of) know what was going on in the cricketing world. I invested in a Grundig Radio so that I could catch international stations. Grundig was a German company founded in 1945. I then would tune to the station that played radio commentary—in the middle of the night (time difference). That, too, catching the channel was an art. I would slowly turn the knob while pressing my ear to the speaker, straining to distinguish between a static noise and the actual commentary. Turn a hair in the wrong direction, and I had missed it. My wife must have thought I'm crazy.

`<Begin confession>`

```
Even now, I'm glued to the TV when a cricket
match is happening. My family has resigned to the
fact that cricket is in my DNA. Whenever I tune
```

to a cricket channel, I see the familiar roll of
eyes and hear the familiar groan.

However, I think I crossed a barrier in my wife's
tolerance when I started to watch women's
cricket.

</End confession>

Chapter Fifteen

My wife had a paternal uncle, Niranjan *kaka*, who lived in New Jersey. He was in his fifties and lived with his wife, Chakshu *kaki*.

```
<Begin clarification>

I do realize the word kaka has a totally
different meaning in other languages. However, it
means father's brother and kaki means father's
brother's wife in Gujarati. Some words in
different languages can mean very different (and
sometimes humorous.)

</End clarification>
```

Over a long weekend, we visited them. We took the subway to 34th Street/Port Authority and changed to an interstate train that would take us to their house. It was a two-storied, single-family, brick house with a side driveway leading to the garage. It was covered in white and surrounded by snow from the previous night. Even the tiny shrubbery surrounding the house was covered in white. It appeared as if a dwarf man in green was wearing a white coat.

We were warmly greeted by a smiling man. I could hear Chakshu *kaki* busy in the kitchen cooking an elaborate meal.

```
<Begin confession>
```

```
I was hoping it would be an authentic Gujarati
meal (vegetarian, of course), and I was not
disappointed.
```

```
</End confession>
```

```
<Begin aside>
```

```
Food is so plentiful in this country that I had
put on a few pounds (okay, quite a few pounds). I
also found the quantity enormous, and there was
(and still is) a lot of wastage. When I was new
to the country and went out to eat, I was amazed
at the amount of food in front of me. I remember
thinking it was for four people. I could hardly
finish a quarter of the quantity. And as time
passed, I noticed that I could finish the plate.
```

```
One of the pet peeves I still have is people
don't finish what's on their plate. When I go out
in a restaurant and see unfinished food on the
table next to me, I just shake my head and think
to myself, no wonder America is the #1 wasteful
country in the world.
```

```
Always remember: waste not, want not.
```

```
</End aside>
```

```
<Begin recycling story>
```
                              * * *

```
Ever since my childhood, recycling has been
ingrained in me. This probably is true for most
of us who grew up in India.

I remember, after reading his newspaper every
morning, my father would place it in a basket.
When the basket started to get full, he would
dial a 'pastiwala.' Within an hour, a man would
come on a black bicycle with a traditional
weighing scale (tarazu). He would place the stack
of newspapers on one plate and the equivalent
weights on the other - adding and subtracting
weights until both sides were balanced. He then
would give my father money in exchange for the
newspapers. He, the pastiwala, would repeat this
several times during the day. When he had
collected enough newspapers, he would take them
to his small shop, where he would sell them to a
larger recycling company. This is not just
limited to pastiwalas. People recycle empty
plastic bottles, tin cans, glass bottles, etc.,
in a similar fashion.

</End recycling story>
```

Theirs was a typical single-family house with a basement
—a standard feature on the East Coast. However, looking
back, when I compare them to the cookie-cutter homes
in California, I find basements on huge properties as
there are no walls around the houses.

After experiencing a totally different life, I was not
looking forward to going to our studio apartment.
Reluctantly, we bade our goodbyes and decided to visit
them soon. We headed back to our Brooklyn apartment.

When I unlocked the door, my mouth fell open when I

saw what was in front of me. The floor had been dug up. The smooth tiles adorning the floor lay broken and scattered on top of a dirt pile, exposing a hole in the ground and a pipe. It had a huge crack. Steam gushed out of it, making a hissing noise. The apartment was super-hot and humid. I asked my wife to stay in the hallway while I ran to the second floor and banged on the building superintendent's[42] door.

I was profusely sweating by now. "What's happening to my apartment?" I yelled.

He narrowed his eyes for a moment, looking confused, and then his expression changed as realization struck. "Oh. You must be from apartment 105."

I was getting angry with his calm demeanor. "That's right. What's going on?" I demanded. "It's been dug up. I can't use it, and I have a pregnant wife."

"Oh, I'm sorry," his voice softened. "There was a leak in the heating pipe. We identified the source where it was. The pipe runs under your apartment. We knocked on the door, but there was no answer. I then had to use the master key to get into your apartment. It was an emergency. The central heating system depends on this pipe. If we had not done anything about it until you returned, none of the units in this building would have any heat."

---

[42] A building superintendent—also known as a super, property manager, or resident manager—oversees maintenance and repairs for a residential building that typically houses 10 or more units.

I was still upset but saw the reasoning in his logic. "Oh, when will it be fixed? I need to live there."

"Two days…three tops," he shrugged nonchalantly. I continued to fume on my way back. My wife was waiting for me in the hallway, looking tired.

"What happened?" she asked.

"Stay here; I'll be right back." I stepped into the hot apartment and quickly called Aruna *masi*. Sweating, I told her my situation.

"Don't worry," she said in a calm voice. "I'll come and get you."

As days passed and my wife's delivery date neared, I realized I had to be around. That meant that I could not travel to other cities. I had to request Donn to find a replacement. So, mustering my courage, I walked to his office and tapped gently on the door. "Knock, knock," I said, although it was wide open. He looked up, and a smile spread across his face.

"Hi, Donn."

"Hi."

"Are you busy?"

"Not really; come in." He waved me in. "Have a seat."

I gingerly walked across and sat in a chair across from him. I looked around.

<Begin confession>

Although I had seen his office many times by now,
it was always a fleeting look, and that too from
outside. This was the first time I was inside his
office.

</End confession>

The walls were unpainted, giving them a natural brick
look. A large glass-top table lay at the center, covered
with yellow folders. He sat in a comfortable swiveling
chair with two more gray chairs across from him. One of
them had a pile of yellow folders. Behind his chair was a
large window that overlooked the street below. A black
bookshelf covered the wall to my right, and a glass side-
table stood flushed to the wall with more yellow folders
on it. I turned my upper torso to look behind. Four
square frames hung. Each one of them had an
amateurish-looking artwork. It appeared as if a little kid
had done it.

He must have seen my half-quizzical expression. "My
daughter did them," he said proudly.

"Ah," I exclaimed. It all made sense now. In the past, I
had seen her in his office on several occasions. Always
doing what little girls did—under the table, playing with
her father's hair while he was busy writing something, and
so on.

He was tremendously patient and always smiling. The
transformation was incredible. Gone was the shrewd and
savvy businessman, to be replaced by a doting daddy to
his little girl.

"How can I help you?" he smiled.

"Well," I hesitated.

"What is it?" his eyes narrowed. "Is there a problem?"

"No, not a problem, really," I quickly shook my head, "it's more like a request?"

He raised his eyebrows, waiting for me to continue. "Yes?"

"It's just that…as you know…my wife is pregnant," I stammered.

"Yes, how is she doing?"

"Very well."

"That's good to hear." He smiled and nodded, waiting for me to say what was on my mind.

"I need to be around her until her delivery," I blurted, unsure of his reaction. *What if he refuses?* I thought. *There's not much I can do about it.* He was thoughtful for a brief moment as he squeezed his upper lip between his index finger and thumb absentmindedly.

He finally smiled. "No problem. I understand. Don't worry. You will be in this office from now on."

```
<Begin confession>

True to his word, he honored his promise. I
haven't gone for another software demonstration
since then.

</End confession>
```

Chapter Sixteen

On a cold winter day in early January, our daughter was born in the general ward at Coney Island Hospital. Earlier in the day, my wife's water broke, and we rushed to the hospital. A few days prior, my mother-in-law had arrived from India to assist my wife (she did the same when our son was born in California).

It was a Thursday morning. I was home as she, our daughter, was overdue. When her water broke, the mother and daughter pair started to panic. Even though I had the same sense of fear inwardly, I had to show that I was in control of my emotions. After all, panic makes you make wrong decisions. I had to think straight and logically. We had our little delivery preparedness bag ready.

```
<Begin tip>
```

No matter how prepared you are, when it's the actual time to deliver, you are unprepared. In my experience, one of the most crucial aspects of a smooth delivery is identifying a person who thinks logically under pressure.

However, it's easier said than done.

</End tip>

Although I, the father, was the wrong candidate to do this, I didn't have much choice. There were only three of us, and my wife was in no condition to make any decisions. That left my mother-in-law and me. And she was new to this country. It would be inconsiderate of me to expect her to make any decisions. I called a cab. We waited for it to arrive in our building's lobby. It was cold and snowing outside. When I saw the yellow taxi pull in front of our building, my mother-in-law and I sandwiched my wife, held her by her arms, and walked gingerly to the cab—taking baby steps.

We were directed to the maternity ward when we arrived at the hospital. It was a massive room with many beds separated by a thin curtain for privacy. Few of the beds were occupied by expectant mothers in various stages of delivery.

As we were about to enter the general delivery ward, we were stopped at the door by a security guard. "Only the parents are allowed in." I asked my mother-in-law to wait outside. I could see anxiety in her eyes, but I assured her that I would regularly come out to update her on her daughter's condition. Unlike other procedures performed at a hospital, where one can approximate the time it would take, this was something that either could take a few minutes or a few hours. And in the worst-case scenario, it could be a Cesarean delivery (C-section.)

Unlike our son's birth, where we had a private room and we were surrounded by multiple nurses, there were no nurses in the general ward, so a midwife delivered her.

<Begin confession>

When my wife went into labor during our son's delivery at Long Beach Children's Hospital in California, I was in New York. She had begged me not to go, but I had dismissed her concerns. "Don't worry. We still have three weeks to go. I'll be back in a few days. Unfortunately, our son decided to come early. I took an early morning flight from LaGuardia Airport to LAX, and it was as though he was waiting for my arrival. He came to this world ten minutes after I arrived.

Before the delivery, when we toured the hospital, they showed us the delivery room. It looked so lovely and picturesque. The bed was perfectly made. The tiny little crib had flowers painted on it. Even the walls had floral wallpapers. Everything looked so neat and tidy in its place.

However, when I entered the room while my wife was delivering our son, it looked like I had just entered a warzone. The bed was unmade, with pillows lying on the floor. Nurses surrounded my wife, urging her to push. My mother-in-law sat in one corner, looking haggard. My wife's friend, Anjali, had come over to help her and looked traumatized.

I remember the look of relief on both my mother-in-law and Anjali as I entered. Of course, my wife was too exhausted to express her anger (that came later).

* * *

`</End confession>`

No matter how much you read, watch on TV, or in a movie about being a father, it doesn't prepare you. The feeling is indescribable. Within a span of a few seconds, you are transformed from being a husband to a father. You are not only responsible for one person but two. I can go on about feelings, but I better stop embarrassing my family.

I remember walking down the wide and empty hallway to convey the good news to my mother-in-law, "*chokri che* (it's a girl.)" She was sitting alone on a long bench, worrying. I informed her that both mother and daughter were doing well. A look of relief spread across her face.

I couldn't help but see the contrast. In India, when a woman was delivering, one would be surrounded by at least a dozen nervous relatives to hear the good news, nervously pacing in the 'delivery waiting room.'

That evening, we took our little bundle of joy home. Niranjan *kaka* and Chakshu *kaki* had driven from New Jersey. I carefully and slowly walked to the car, as I didn't want to slip on the pavement holding a newborn. I had tightly bundled her with multiple layers to protect her from the cold weather.

Fortunately, that was the only winter I spent in New York. After the initial novelty of witnessing snow for the very first time in life had worn off, I found it to be a nuisance.

Coming from Mumbai, I hated the cold weather. In addition, I would have to bundle myself even if it was a quick milk-run. On top of that, I would keep having to take my jacket off when I was in the building or a subway (they all are heated) and put them back again when I would step out. Even if that weren't a big task, I would wear thermals (I know, I know, I sound like an idiot, but hey, remember, I come from Mumbai.)

I was ready for a change.

Chapter Seventeen

DBC relocated its office from New York to Florida in the late spring/early summer of 1990. I was elated. I had been to Florida once before and was surprised. When my plane landed and I came out of the conveyor tunnel, it felt like I was entering a paradise through a magical portal. I couldn't imagine the stark difference between the two cities on the same coast. Gone was the gloomy city with gray skies, and here was a blue sky and sunshine.

Many folks escape to Florida during winter. It's not just known for its warm climate, beautiful beaches, and many golf resorts, but it also has many theme parks and water parks. In addition, it's a favorite state to live in once folks retire. Many people prefer to migrate there to avoid the bitter winter in the northern states. It also is a favorite state among college students to have their Spring Break. For a week or so, many coastal cities and beaches are filled with skimpily clad girls in their bikinis and young men in shorts—showing off their six-packs. During that week, finding a room in a hotel is next to impossible.

Many such rooms—meant to accommodate two people —are occupied by many more students. It's a sight to behold.

Aruna *masi* and Chandrakant *masa* had come to our apartment on our last day in New York. Our daughter was four-month-old by then. Although I was sad to say goodbye to them, I was very excited to go to a warmer climate.

```
<Begin walk down the memory lane>

During our brief stay in New York, they have
helped us so much. Knowing how expensive a
medical checkup would be to someone like us who
had very little money, Paresh would drop in
regularly to check how our daughter was
progressing.

Once, he took us to the nearest mall to get our
daughter's ears pierced. He was carrying her, and
she was looking around with wide eyes and smiling
randomly. Paresh looked at her and laughed, "you
have no idea what's coming to you, right?" She
continued grinning, not understanding what he was
saying.

</End walk down the memory lane>
```

Our office was in the city of Boca Raton in Palm Beach County. It was one of the wealthy cities with an upscale shopping center. It also boasted the largest indoor mall in Palm Beach County. We, the three of us, flew with Pankaj (who has now settled in Sydney, Australia, and has a thriving AS/400 business) and Ram C. Both, light-eyed

Pankaj and scrawny Ram C. Were my colleagues at DBC in New York. By the way, when we were in New York, Pankaj was the only person who drove to work in a car. I used to envy him then; however, I'm not too sure now as I see the bumper-to-bumper New York traffic (similar to L.A. or Mumbai). Just like in Mumbai, if one had to reach their destination in time, they preferred to take the subway.

Talking about Ram C., there is a little story behind us calling him Ram C. Back in New York, we had three people with the same first name of Ram. Whenever someone said, "hey, Ram," all of them would look up. To solve this, we addressed them by adding their last name. So, we had Ram C., Ram N., and Ram S.

We flew into Fort Lauderdale Airport, Florida, from LaGuardia, New York, and rented a car (Pankaj being the only driver. None of the others had a license to drive in the U.S. Although I have driven in India, it's way too different. To begin with, we drive on the other side of the road, and the rules are different and strictly enforced. Also, I've always driven a stick shift.)

```
<Begin confession>
```

```
If you have not driven a stick shift, you don't
realize how blessed you are to drive an
automatic. A stick shift requires the skill to
control three pedals instead of two. In addition
to one for the brake and one for the gas, you
have a clutch. It may sound very trivial - so
long as you are driving on a straight road.
However, if you are going on a slope and you have
```

to apply brakes to stop the vehicle, God help you. It's a balancing act, an art, a skill that is very difficult to master. You have to put one foot on the gas pedal while the toe part of your other foot is on the gas pedal and the heel on the brake pedel.

Moreover, as you perform this circus act, you must apply the correct pressure. A little more on the gas, and you bump into the car in front of you, a little less, and the engine stalls. And if it does, you must remember to shift your gear to neutral before restarting the engine.

Those who have driven on Mumbai roads will be able to relate to my traumatic experience… especially those who have driven on Peddar Road near Jaslok Hospital (I know, way too specific. For ABCDs, think of driving a stick shift in San Francisco.)

</End confession>

* * *

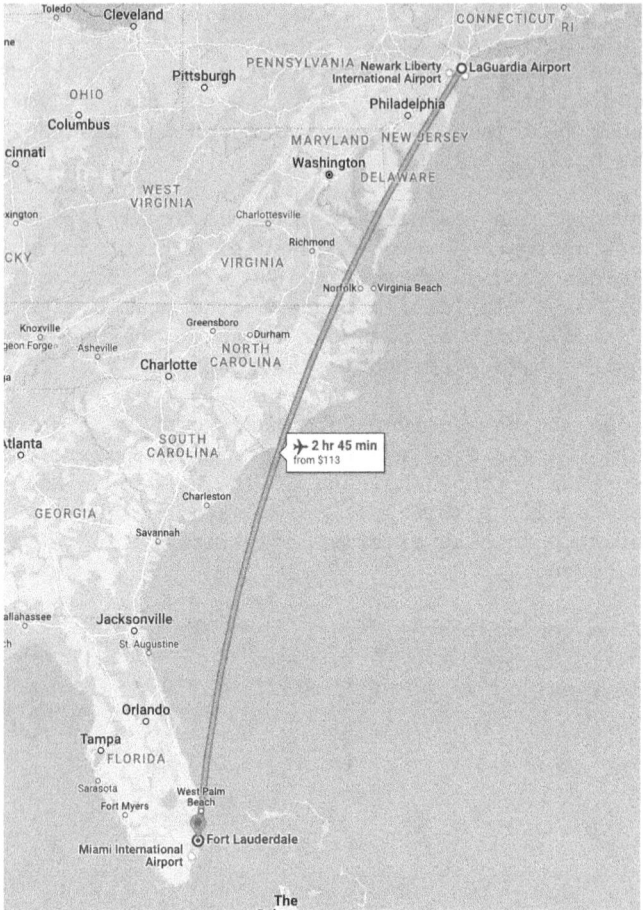

The hotel was a tall building with an open courtyard with a fountain in the center. A glass ceiling acted as the roof high above. Sun rays seeped through it to reach the bottom. A few comfortable-looking couches lay in the courtyard's center with floral arrangements next to them. A glass elevator ran up and down on one side, enabling its occupants to have a look down below.

After checking in, we got into the car and drove around to explore the city. We went on I95, the main highway, and crossed over to the famous A1A[43], which ran parallel to I95 and was separated by water.

We were fascinated by the vast drawbridges that enabled the vehicles to cross the waterway when down and allowed million-dollar yachts to cross the channel when they were drawn up.

After dinner at an Indian restaurant, we returned to our hotel in the evening.

---

[43] State Road A1A (SR A1A) is a major north–south Florida State Road that runs 338.752 miles (545.168 km) along the Atlantic Ocean, from Key West at the southern tip of Florida, to Fernandina Beach, just south of Georgia on Amelia Island. It is the main road through most oceanfront towns. Part of SR A1A is designated the A1A Scenic and Historic Coastal Byway. Source: Wikipedia.

Chapter Eighteen

We were given a few days off to look for an apartment and settle in. We saw several close to our office—so we didn't have to drive—or so we thought, but we were in for a rude awakening. America is a massive country with plenty of open lands; thus, the buildings are spread apart. Once you leave a busy metropolitan city as New York, gone are the closely huddled skyscrapers. Most structures are two to three stories with a vast parking lot surrounding them. Many times, one will prefer driving to the next building rather than walking.

```
<Begin rant>

Apart from cities such as New York, Chicago, San
Francisco, and many others that have a sound
transit system, public transportation in the US
sucks. In a sprawling metropolis like Los
Angeles, one is severely handicapped without a
vehicle.

</End rant>
```

* * *

```
<Begin a Los Angeles trivia>

I reside in a city located in the southern corner
of Los Angeles Metro area, and my friend, Shiva,
lives in a town in a corner in the north. We are
separated by over fifty miles (around eighty
kilometers). However, the distance doesn't deter
us. We are used to traveling long distances now.

Los Angeles is notorious for its traffic. We have
the most complex network of freeways. So much so
that it has become a conversation starter. It's
very common to hear someone giving a tip on which
route is the best to reach a particular
destination.

I suspect many visitors from India skip Los
Angeles for the vast distances between the two
destinations.

</End a Los Angeles trivia>
```

Once again, I digress. Coming back to my apartment search, I rejected many—too small, not within my budget (by now, I was absorbed as a full-time employee of DBC, and my income had more than doubled; however, Boca Raton is a costly city to live in, with golf courses, big mansions, pretty lakes and ponds (we were warned not to venture in lakes or ponds as they could have alligators.) After all, Florida is a gator country with around 1.3 million of them. It's common to see them in the least unexpected places: swimming pools, golf courses, roads, and many more.

* * *

We went to the office to get some advice from the secretary (who was a local woman). "There's nothing you'll find within your price range anywhere nearby. You will have to widen your search area," she said. "Palm Beach is an expensive county with many millionaires and billionaires. Broward country is much more affordable." We took her advice and started to look for apartments in other cities, asking her about them. She rejected a few of them before agreeing to our choice. North Lauderdale.

Once we had decided on the city, our next task was to find an apartment that met our budget. By now, we had resigned to the fact that no matter where we stayed, we had to drive to our office. Even if we had found something in Palm Beach County, we would be driving to and fro our work to our apartment.

Our apartment complex was a well-maintained cluster of several three-storied buildings with red-tiled roofs and a beige stucco exterior. Each building had its own swimming pool. The main building housed an administrative office and a large swimming pool. The complex also had additional amenities such as a gymnasium, a laundromat, a jacuzzi adjacent to the swimming pool, etc. We were impressed, but were happier when we found out how much it would cost us monthly —$600 for a two-bedroom unit (including the utilities). *I can afford it,* I thought, quickly calculating my other expenses.

I looked at the others. They, too, seemed to like what they saw. The manager took us in a white electric golf cart to show us the property. I sat next to her while the others sat in the backseat with our daughter in my wife's lap. She stopped at several locations as she explained the facilities on the property. She also told us that our apartment complex was situated near a huge grocery store that was open 24 hours. "Also, we are close to the Everglades[44]."

"What are they?" I asked.

"It's a natural marshland consisting of several species of wildlife."

"Oh, I see," I nodded.

I then turned around to face the others. "What do you think, guys?" They nodded their approval.

"We'll take it," I told the property manager.

"Excellent. I'll get the paperwork started," she smiled as she navigated the golf cart. When we reached the rental office, she showed us a miniature model of the property.

"We are here," she tapped on one of the buildings.

I chose an apartment in the farthest building. Ram C. and Pankaj decided on one on the ground floor, overlooking an artificial lake with a fountain in the middle and several ducks paddling around. Their apartment was such that one could slide open the glass doors of their living room and walk a few feet down a pebbled slope to reach the lake. We rented two 2-bedroom units: one for

---

[44] The Everglades is a natural region of tropical wetlands in the southern portion of the U.S. state of Florida. Source: Wikipedia.

my family and the other to be shared between Ram C. and Pankaj.

We spent the next few days between going into the office and leaving early to settle our new apartment. Our boxes had arrived from New York in an 18-wheeler—along with the office boxes. We, of course, had very few boxes. We realized how little we had when we unpacked them and placed our belongings in the apartment. We had hardly filled ten to fifteen percent of the total area of our apartment. It still looked barren, devoid of any furniture.

I then remembered the office manager suggesting we drive around the neighborhood. "Be on the lookout for a yard sale. You will be able to furnish your apartment at a throwaway price." So, we scoped our neighborhood over the weekend. We stopped at the first yard sale sign. We were amazed at the different pieces of furniture we were able to get our hands on at a—as the office manager said, throwaway price. After all, one person's junk is another person's treasure.

We furnished the apartment with a dining table, a showcase from a yard sale, an inexpensive mattress (without the bedframe), and a maroon sofa from the clearance section of a furniture shop.

My wife got busy transforming an apartment into a home.

Chapter Nineteen

Our office was twenty-two miles north of our apartments. We would go north on the busy I95. Fortunately, since we were three in the car (Pankaj, Ram C., and I), we could drive in the carpool lane, allowing us to zoom past the heavy traffic of single drivers occupying four lanes.

Unfortunately, this arrangement didn't last for long. Soon, Pankaj left for India. I had to get my driving license and, more importantly, a car within my budget. Like all Indian FOBs, I narrowed it down to a Honda or a Toyota. I went to the Honda's car dealership. After several back-and-forths of passing a piece of paper and the salesman going to his manager's cabin to get a new amount, he finally slid me the piece of paper with a reasonable amount. I, however, was not convinced. "I have to make a call to my financial adviser." The salesman looked exasperated but wanted to close the deal. By now, he had already spent over four hours. Reluctantly, he agreed. He slid the phone instrument across the smooth table. I picked up the receiver and dialed my 'financial adviser.' Of course, he didn't know my financial adviser was my friend, Arun. He worked at DBC when I was in New York. He and Pankaj shared an apartment there.

```
<Begin aside>
```

Once, Arun narrated a story I thought was amusing. I hope, my dear reader, you find it funny too.
When he was a student at the University of Florida at Gainesville, a fellow student had recently arrived from India (super-fresh FOB). Coming from a small town in India, he wasn't comfortable with English-lingo and its nuances.
One day, Arun and a few of his friends (including super-fresh FOB) made a road trip to New Orleans in the neighboring state of Louisiana. They wanted to visit the famous French Quarter during Mardi Gras. After participating in the festivities until the wee hours, they decided to stop for a drink in a bar. As they were walking toward the bar, they came across a prostitute. Everyone but the super-fresh FOB knew who she was and what she did. She saw the poor lad staring at her, checking out her skimpy outfit. She smiled at him. "Hey, honey."
The lad replied while gawking, "Hi." He still was unaware of her profession.
She smiled coyly. "Can I help you with anything?"
"Like?"
"Anything…a hand job, a blow job, anything you want."
"No," the lad shook his head. "So nice of you to offer me a job, but I already have a university assistantship."

```
</End aside>
```

* * *

He was sent to several client sites and was now at a site in Tampa, Florida. He had been in the country for a few years as a student; hence, he was our go-to guy.

He answered the phone after a few rings and asked me to shave another $500 from the asking price.

The salesman was studying my face as he didn't understand Hindi. He only could pick up words such as dollars, too much, etc.

```
<Begin trivia>

Many of us speak in Hinglish, a combination of
Hindi and English. This is not unique to us. I've
heard people speaking in Spanglish
(Spanish+English).

Of course, Hinglish is spoken by those who know
Hindi. There are many here who don't know the
language. Even when they watch a Bollywood movie,
they turn on the subtitles.

</End trivia>
```

There were many Indians in my office who didn't speak Hindi (or spoke broken Hindi). Fortunately, Arun was not one of them.

"Well," he asked eagerly when I disconnected. I looked at him and shook my head. "No."

"*What?*" he looked at me exasperatedly, throwing his hands. I could see that I was trying his patience. "What is the problem now?"

"The price is a little higher than we can pay."

"How much higher?"

"By $500."

"Okay," he closed his eyes and pinched his nose. He then opened them, took a deep breath, and looked at me. "So, you are saying that if I lower the price by $500, you'll buy the car tonight."

"Most probably," I said smugly. I was enjoying this.

"I need to get it approved by my manager," he said as he got up from his chair. "I'll be right back."

Momentarily, he reappeared. "Good news, my manager agreed. But this is his final offer."

I looked at my wife. Our daughter was playing in her lap. She looked at me and nodded her approval.

"Yes," I told the car salesman.

"Great," he clapped. A look of relief spread across his face. He got up and shook my hand. "Congratulations. I'll be back with the paperwork."

After spending another hour signing the paperwork, we drove out with a brand new Honda Civic. Red.

Owning a vehicle not only meant convenience to go to work; rather, it symbolized freedom.

We got busy settling down and filling our pantries with various Indian spices and our refrigerator with Indian vegetables. Back in New York, we had a large Indian population with several grocery stores to choose from. Many of them carried fruits and vegetables very commonly found in India. However, they were not available in the big grocery chains here in Florida. Many chains have them in 2022, but I'm talking about 1990.

However, this was Florida. We didn't have our 'Indian strip.' We were hundreds of miles away from Jackson Heights in Queens, where many Indians shopped. We were in for a rude awakening. Finally, we found an Indian grocery store very far from us. Moreover, it was stocked with fruits and vegetables that appeared a few days old. When my wife complained about it, the shopkeeper merely shrugged. "The Indian population is relatively small. We get a limited supply of our stock from New York. There's nothing I can do about it. Sorry."

The message was clear - take it or leave it.

*_*_*

Miami was south of us and has a substantial population of Cuban immigrants. If any other ethnicity looks closest to Indians, it's the Cubans. There were several instances when I was mistaken as a Cuban, and the opposite person started speaking in Spanish.

```
<Begin confession>

Although I've lived in Los Angeles since 1992,
I'm ashamed to admit that I don't know the
language that is so widely spoken here. Someday,
I intend to remedy this. Until then, I rely on my
trusted Google Translate.

</End confession>
```

I only knew one sentence, thanks to my friend, Subra. "no hablo español."

```
<Begin geographical trivia>
```

Cuba is merely ninety miles south of the southernmost tip of Florida, the beautiful island of Key West. I was fortunate to visit the famous marker.

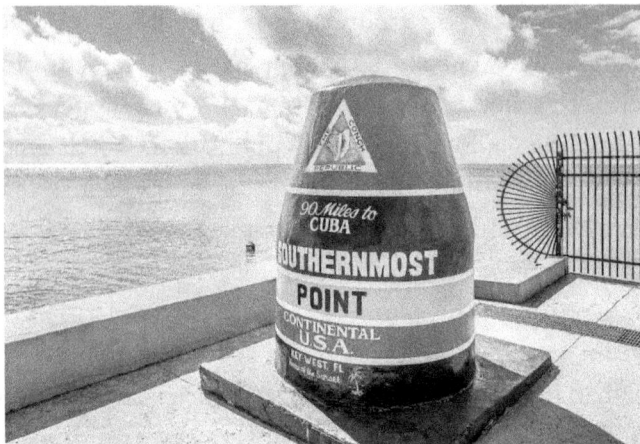

It's difficult to comprehend the stark difference between the two countries—one being capitalist and the other being communist. They are so close geographically yet so far apart in their philosophy.

At the risk of sounding like a spokesperson for Florida Tourism, driving from Miami to Key West is one of the most memorable journeys I've embarked on. It should be a must-do on your bucket list.

</End geographical trivia>

Chapter Twenty

After a few months, my friend, Rajiv, visited us with his mother. He was studying civil engineering at the University of Tennessee at Chattanooga (UTC). Rajiv is my childhood friend. We studied at the same school in Mumbai (Sanskar Jyot). He and my younger brother were classmates. He lived in the next building.

<Begin a walk down memory lane>

Back in 1977, when it was announced that Star Wars was coming to a movie hall (Sterling Cinema), we were extremely thrilled. However, Sterling Cinema was downtown, and we lived in the suburbs. Moreover, we wanted to see Star Wars on the first show on the day it was released (a Friday). Back then, we had the concept of 'Advance Booking.' Hence, to purchase a ticket for Friday's show, one had to book it on a Monday. We decided to go by a local train on Monday. We, Rajiv, Mukesh (another childhood friend who lives in India) and I, got up at 4 am and went to the local station to get on a train that would take us downtown. After getting off at the last station (Churchgate), we walked across the vast cricket ground (*Azad Maidan*), where many practiced cricket in nets—honing their skills.

Our excitement rose as we neared Sterling Cinema, and our pace quickened. However, when we turned the corner, we groaned in dismay to see a long queue had already formed. If we went to the end of the line, there was no way we would be able to see the movie on Friday. All the tickets would be sold by then. We also were aware of scalpers buying a significant chunk of them so that they could sell them at a higher price on Friday. Star Wars had generated so much buzz that everyone was anticipating it to be a major hit.

We had only one option left. Cut in the line. Even then, it took us six to eight hours before we got our turn. Am I proud of it? Absolutely not. Am I glad I did it? Absolutely.

That's how I saw Star Wars on the day it was released in India. And, it was totally worth getting up early in the morning, taking a train ride, and cutting in the queue.

</End of a walk down memory lane>

There are way too many stories from my childhood that I can narrate. But you, my dear reader, would not be able to relate to them; hence, suffice to say that he is a very good friend. However, we have one thing in common—our love for cricket. Just like me, he's a huge cricket fan and loves the Mumbai Indians. When I was a young boy, we invested in a cricket kit: pads, gloves, a season ball[45], and a

---

[45] A season ball (cricket ball) is a hard, solid ball used to play cricket. A cricket ball consists of a cork core wound

crotch guard. He also happened to be a team member of The Juniors (remember the cricket team that The Seniors could never defeat?)

---

with string then a leather cover stitched on, and manufacture is regulated by cricket law at first-class level. Cricket balls are harder and heavier than baseballs.

Injuries and fatalities have been caused by cricket balls during matches.The hazards posed by cricket balls were a key motivator for the introduction of protective equipment.

Source: Wikipedia.

ANATOMY OF CRICKET BALL

Stitching :
To join the leather parts, stitching
isdone of two parts of Leather.

Inner Core :
Inner Core is made of high
quality cork material and
thread on top of it

UPPER MATERIAL :
Made of High Quality Leather,
Alum Tanned is the Process of
Cleaning the Leather

His mother was visiting him from India. He called me one evening, and I was delighted to hear his voice. After taking a brief walk down the memory lane of our good-old-days-in-Mumbai, we decided that they would fly down, and then all of us would drive up north to Disney World in Orlando.

When they arrived, we spent a few days touring our surroundings in our brand new car that I was showing off. However, looking back, I realize how foolish I must have looked. That's because the very first time I drove a car in this country (yes, without a license. But only in an empty parking lot) was at Rajiv's house in Chattanooga. On one of my trips with Donn, I had flown to nearby Atlanta. Once we were done with our presentation, I took a brief detour to his house before heading back to New York. He was driving a huge Mercedes-Benz. He knew how much I loved driving. He took me to an empty parking lot and let me take the wheel. I must say that there is a stark difference between driving a non-powered vehicle (which I drove in India) and a powered one here. I found the steering wheel, the accelerator, and the brake pedals to be hyper-sensitive.

"Slowly," Rajiv warned me. I tapped on the gas pedal, and the car lurched forward. Terrified, I hit the brakes. Rajiv almost banged his face on the dashboard.

"What are you doing?" he laughed. "I said slowly. Cars here are very different from the ones you have driven in India. Try again. Slowly, this time." However, I was too afraid to drive anymore. Fearing I would bang his car, I let him get behind the wheel.

That was my brief introduction to driving on American roads.

--*

Disney World was about two hundred miles north of our apartment. It's about three hours of a drive on Florida's Turnpike. We had a wonderful time there. Rajiv's mother doted over our daughter, pushing her stroller throughout the day, fussing over her all the time, and swiping away her hair that covered her eyes.

```
<Begin confession>
```

All my DBC friends were bachelors. Hence, our daughter had the privilege of being spoiled by many single uncles. All of them are married with adult sons and daughters now. However, our daughter had a special place in their heart.

I'm fortunate to still have Sanjay, Ram C, and Arun live nearby. They have been with me on my journey from my early days in New York to Florida and are now with me in Los Angeles. In addition to them, I have other friends who were with me during my struggling days and have now settled in different parts of the US and the world. Although they are physically far away, it has become a breeze to keep in touch with them via WhatsApp.

```
</End confession>
```

I remember, when I visited Rajiv with my family after a few months; our daughter took her very first steps. After graduating, he returned to India and now has a thriving business. When he visits me now, we catch up on childhood memories and our lives in America.

Also, he being a strict vegetarian (like my wife) makes it easy to follow his dietary requirements. Although nowadays, it has become easier to be a vegetarian, it's still challenging to explain the concept to a non-Jain. "Yes, we eat dairy but not eggs. Cheese and milk are fine."

```
<Begin various flavors of vegetarianism>
```

Being a vegetarian is way too complex in India. However, the primary reason is religion. While some Hindu vegetarians consume dairy products—but no eggs, the other Hindus consume dairy products—including eggs. And most Jains eat dairy—excluding eggs, but no vegetables that grow underground such as potatoes, carrots, garlic, onions, etc. On the other hand, there are some Hindus that consume seafood. Many Asian countries treat seafood as a vegetarian diet.

I hope your confusion is crystal clear now.

</End various flavors of vegetarianism>

Chapter Twenty-One

Our office at Boca Raton was in a sprawling business park. It was a cluster of several single story buildings with individual units. Each office building was a U-shaped structure, with the front being the bottom of the U and the top being the back side of the building (more like an inverted U).

I had already obtained my driving license by then. So did Ram C. He, too, had bought a brand-new maroon Toyota Corolla. We would alternate between his car and mine while commuting to work. Since the three of us worked at the same office, it was easy to drive together— a significant advantage in using the carpool lane.

The front part of the office was for visitors, and Donn's office had the secretary's room next to his. It was followed by a small conference room and a tiny kitchen area opposite it, separated by a corridor that led to the programmers' area.

My desk was situated on the back side of the unit. A gray partition further separated it from other programmers sitting in their cubicles. Tall windows (running from floor to ceiling and tinted to keep the beating Florida sun out) kept our office cool. Near the cubicles was a long table with eight chairs we used for having our breakfast or lunch.

Every morning at ten, we would hear the melodious honk of a food truck. It was called the roach-coach, dashing between several buildings. The driver would swing open the side to reveal the contents he was selling: coffee, sandwiches, bagels, etc. He would announce his arrival by honking several times, many times, honking as he approached. He would park his truck for less than five minutes, and people from different units would pour out to buy things. Once done, he would close shop and drive away to the next destination.

The same food truck would make its round in the afternoon during our lunch hours. However, there would be fewer customers this time.

Unlike the fancy food trucks nowadays, they were much smaller with minimal things to sell. Many of them now have an app where the younger generation tracks it on the phone, so they know how far it is from them. Back then, our app was the melodious honk. I would buy a coffee from it daily and enjoy it at my desk.

Lunch would usually be a sandwich my wife made and a bottle of apple juice.

<Begin description of an Indian sandwich>

The Indian sandwich is totally different from the

ones available here. They consist of a green
chutney spread, thinly sliced tomatoes, potatoes,
and cucumber with a sprinkle of sandwich powder.
The ingredients can vary depending upon personal
preference, and so can the chutney spread.
However, when one says Indian sandwich, they mean
a vegetarian sandwich.

</End description of an Indian sandwich>

By now, I had moved up the success ladder of owning a car, so I had ditched the briefcase. We all used to have our lunch on the table. After lunch, Bharat (who had recently joined DBC), Ram C., and I used to go around the pond for a walk.

We had a large pond in front of our office with a concrete walkway around its edges shaded by tall palm trees. The pond was at a lower level than the walkway, with a gentle slope of perfectly manicured grass. Both Ram C. and I were smokers back then. We would leisurely stroll around the pond while enjoying an after-lunch cigarette.

Daily on our walk, we always saw an alligator on the slope. It was sunbathing with its mouth open. Initially, we found it scary; however, we got used to its presence.

<Begin warning>

If you have never come across an alligator
sunbathing, here's a piece of advice. They stay
still like a statue. One would make the mistake
of going near them. It's then when they strike.
And their grip is like an iron cage has clanged
on you. Once they get hold of their prey, they
drag it down to the bottom of the pond to do a

death-roll where they rotate their bodies several times.

So, please be extra careful and don't try your heroics (or, as they say in Hindi, *heropanti*).

</End warning>

--*

When we returned home, we would visit each other's apartment many evenings to have dinner together. By now, Arun and Sanjay had joined us, and so had my other friends. When we got together, it was a full house. In addition, I had made a few new friends. Occasionally, I'd meet them too.

To my delight, I had joined a local cricket club. Florida being close to the Caribbean, there is a large population of them. Like India, they too love cricket (after all, they too were a British colony. Most of the cricket-playing nations are ex-British colonies. As we joke many times, two gifts from them were English and cricket.)

Even though my stay in Florida was short, it was memorable. The weather, too, was very similar to Mumbai—hot and muggy. It would rain frequently. The only thing I was not used to was the sudden change in the weather. One minute, it would be bright and sunny with clear blue skies, and the next, it would become dark and cloudy with heavy rains. And the next minute, the showers would pass, making way to clear blue sky as if nothing had happened. I remember it happened to me once when I was driving on the freeway. It turned dark without any warning. It began to rain heavily. The visibility became so bad that I had to pull my vehicle to the side of the freeway and wait till the thunderstorm passed. It was an unnerving experience for me but, a regular occurrence for Floridians.

Looking back, I visited many places in my trusted Honda Civic. I drove all the way up to Orlando and down to Key West. I went east to Cape Canaveral to visit NASA at the Kennedy Space Center and west to Tampa (when I visited Arun.)

Even now, after so many years in L.A., I have fond memories of Florida.

Chapter Twenty-Two

One day when I was busy hacking at my keyboard, I heard the office secretary's voice. "This is your desk." The cubicle next to me had remained empty since we moved into our new office. It had been used to keep old files and manuals on the desk now. Since mine was a corner cubicle, I was surrounded by walls behind me and one to my right. Curious, I slid my chair and peeked past the dividing partition on my left. I saw the secretary clearing the desk, stacking those files and manuals in her hands. "I'll let you settle in," she continued as she cocked her head toward the phone, "call me if you need anything."

"Thank you." A portly man stood there holding a black briefcase. He had salt-n-pepper hair that was closely cut. His face was round with chubby cheeks. He sported a thin mustache.

He placed his briefcase on the table and looked around, surveying his cubicle.

"Hi," I said. He turned his head to look at me and smiled, "Hi." I proffered my hand and introduced myself.

He shook it while smiling, "I'm Ashok Arora."

Upon hearing his name, a head popped up above my cubicle. It was Ram C. "Ashok Arora? Did you say, Ashok Arora?"

"Yes," he nodded.

"The Ashok Arora?"

He laughed. "I don't know what you mean by 'The Ashok Arora.'"

"Oh, don't be so modest," Ram C. Continued, "aren't you one of the founders of Infosys?"

"That's right," he smiled. "That's me."

"I don't believe it," his eyes widened.

I was highly impressed now. To sit beside one of the founders of Infosys was an honor. It was a very rare privilege. *Wait till I tell her,* I was thinking of impressing my wife that evening.

"Nice to meet you, Ashok," I said casually, not wanting to sound like a geeky fan. "I'm sitting right next to you. Holler if you need anything."

"I will, thank you," he nodded as he switched on his terminal. The familiar green sign-on screen flickered to life. He looked at me and said, "I'll need my credentials to sign in."

"Oh, right. Of course," I eagerly nodded and looked at Ram C., "he will set you up. He has the proper authority."

"Sure," Ram C. nodded. His head disappeared as he sat in his chair. Momentarily, I heard the familiar clicks of the keyboard. His head reappeared, this time with an additional limb—his arm. He held a piece of paper.

"Here you go." He handed it to Ashok. "Thank you," he nodded.

He proceeded to settle down in his new cubicle, getting familiarized with his surroundings. I showed him around, not that there was much to show. He had spent a few minutes with Donn (in his office) before coming to the back side. I informed him about the timings for the food truck. "It's here for just five minutes before it drives away to its next destination."

"Oh, okay," he nodded.

"I usually get only coffee. But it also carries some good breakfast sandwiches."

"Good to know. Is there anything else I should know?"

"You know where the kitchen is, right?" I pointed to the tiny room.

"Yes."

"As you can see, it's not big. We have a small refrigerator, a microwave, and a coffee machine."

I pointed to the table. "We have our lunch here. After that, we like to go for a stroll around the pond. You must have noticed it, right?"

"Yes," he nodded.

"You are welcome to join us."

"Thank you."

From that day on, he would join us occasionally.

*_*_*

As days passed, Ashok and I got to know each other. In addition to learning programming techniques, I also looked forward to him narrating his experiences at

Infosys. I invited him to join us for dinner at my apartment. He then reciprocated by inviting us all to his bachelor's apartment for a pizza party.

After a few months, he was gone. When I inquired about him with the secretary, I was informed that he had resigned and left Florida. No goodbyes, no contact info, no keeping in touch, etc. Just a poof.

That was the last time I saw him. Although it was for a brief while, I cherished the time we spent together.

Looking back, when I tell folks that one of the founders of Infosys was sitting next to me and programming, they courteously nod, but I can see in their eyes that they are thinking, "he's fibbing."

```
<Begin confession>

I've searched for him on the Internet. I've
googled him (to back my story) but to no avail.

</End confession>
```

*_*_*

IBM had its offices in Palm Beach. Although we didn't use their facilities to demonstrate our software a lot, I would drive there (with my bulky spool tapes) to load it on the previous day. I would enjoy driving in Florida on a clear day.

Sometimes, when returning home, I would drive on the surface streets instead of taking the freeway, especially when it was raining. I would enjoy the lush green golf courses dotted with ponds and sand traps. Even when it was raining, I would spot diehard golfers teeing off, lugging their golf bags on the fairway, navigating their white golf carts on the winding pathway, or leaning on their clubs on putting greens—patiently awaiting their turn.

```
<Begin confession>
```

```
Rains would whisk me back to the monsoons of
Mumbai. The steaming hot cup of chai (tea) with
hot bhajjis (fritters). Walking to Juhu Beach and
eating hot bhuttas (corn in a husk) grilled on an
open flame and then splashed with lime dabbed in
a mixture of salt and chili powder. Trekking on
my favorite hill station, Matheran, with water
gushing down the lush green mountains surrounding
me.
```

```
</End confession>
```

When I would return home, I'd try to recreate the magic by having a hot cup of tea and eating my favorite snacks; however, it was not the same.

Some things can never be replaced—no matter how hard you try.

Chapter Twenty-Three

After about a year and a half of our stay in Florida (where I explored many parts of the state, visited my friend Arun—who lived in Clearwater—with Sanjay and Ram C., went to the Everglades, toured the world-famous South Beach in Miami, drove through the Florida Keys to Key West[46], and many other touristy things), CAMP was sold to a company, Leadtech, in Los Angeles, California. We (five programmers) came as a 'package deal.' A man, Mr.R. (name withheld for privacy), flew down to interview us. In his fifties, he had curly hair, perfectly tanned skin, and a friendly smile. He was thin with long legs. He wore a black leather jacket and a black shirt with

---

[46] The Florida Keys are a coral cay archipelago located off the southern coast of Florida, forming the southernmost part of the continental United States. They begin at the southeastern coast of the Florida peninsula, about 15 miles (24 km) south of Miami, and extend in a gentle arc south-southwest and then westward to Key West. Source: Wikipedia.

two buttons open. A thick gold chain that shone rested on his chest.

I was the first to be interviewed. I entered the conference room with a big smile. He got up from his chair and extended his hand across the table, "Hi, I'm Mr.R." He had a soft but clear voice. I leaned across and shook it, "hi." His hand was supple but firm. He gestured at one of the chairs. "Have a seat." He did the same. We sat across from each other. He leaned back in his chair and looked over his tiny gold-rimmed glasses. "So, tell me about yourself."

"Well…," I started narrating my accomplishments and specialties. He listened to me attentively, occasionally nodding and interrupting me to ask a question.

```
<Begin confession>

Looking back, I realize it was not an interview;
but a mere formality. He had already bought the
CAMP software. He wanted to gauge where I would
fit in his company.
As many who have worked here can attest, working
culture is vastly different between the two
coasts. The attitude towards work on the West
Coast is more laid back. Seeing employees coming
to their places of work in shorts and tee shirts
is ubiquitous. On the other hand, the East Coast
is more formal.

Personally, I think the weather plays a large
part in one's attire. When my friends visit me
from the east coast during 'winter' (it being
mild in Southern California), I am astonished to
see them going out in shorts and tee shirts,
whereas I am bundled up in my winter clothes.
```

They make fun of me, but hey, in my defense, this
is the only season we get to wear warm clothes.

</End confession>

Thankfully, he had removed his jacket and hung it over
the back of his chair. *Who wears a leather jacket in this heat?* I
thought.

I didn't know then that he had come in directly from
the airport. And while traveling in a plane, the
temperatures are much cooler.

<Begin confession>

While traveling to India, I always wear a jacket
over a thick, full-sleeved shirt. I wear socks on
my feet (which I never take off throughout my
twenty-four-hour journey.) As soon as I'm seated,
I cover my ears with headphones with the other
end left uninserted into the sound port. I'm sure
the person sitting next to me might think I'm
crazy. But do I care? No way. I just want to be
comfortable.

</End confession>

"Do you have any questions for me?" he asked.

"Yes," I nodded. "What's the dress code?"

"Oh," he smiled, "business casual."

"That means no ties, right?"

"Correct," he laughed.

I was chosen to join my new office in Los Angeles. We
spent the next few days (and nights) at home boxing our
wares. The last few days in Florida were very hectic and

stressful as we had just a finite time before the shipper came to our apartment to collect our boxes. I also found a shipper to transport my car (something I'd need on day one.)

"You can get a rental for a few days, but eventually, you'll need a car," Mr.R. had warned me. "Also, once you settle down, you'll have to apply for your California driving license and get a new set of plates."

"Oh," I had said.

```
<Begin confession>

When I got my California plates, I paid extra for
vanity plates in our daughter's name.

Now I think it's the FOBbiest thing to do.
However, it's just a personal opinion. To each
their own.

</End confession>
```

We were booked on a nonstop flight from Fort Lauderdale to LAX—one of the busiest airports in the world. We would be taking off at 10 A.M., and since California is three hours behind Florida, it would be 7 A.M. local time there.

And to make matters worse, our daughter was running a temperature. Hence, we would have to find a doctor as soon as we landed. Air travel creates havoc on little children with fevers and ear infections. Throughout our long plane ride, she was highly uncomfortable.

We had a memorable time in Florida, but it was time to

move on. We didn't know what the future held. Also, we knew very little about California. To us, it was a faraway mystical land famous for surfers, beaches, Hollywood, and Silicon Valley.

```
<Begin confession>
```

```
Now, having been here since 1992, I can sing
praises about, boast of how big it is, how
beautiful the landscape and the beaches are, and
how beautiful some of the waiters and waitresses
are (they come here to try their luck in the
entertainment industry, but most of them end up
waiting tables to pay their bills.) However, to
me, California is home. Sure, we have our share
of natural disasters and are often victims of
Mother Nature's fury. But it's totally worth it.
Also, having lived in a city near the sea all my
life now gives me psychological comfort. My
current house is very close to the Pacific ocean.
I often go for a drive along the Pacific Coast
Highway or to the beach to watch the sunset.
```

```
Yes, I'm very fortunate to live in California.
```

```
</End Confession>
```

```
<Begin touring tip>
```

```
There's more to see and visit in California than
Los Angeles, San Diego, San Francisco, Napa
Valley, and Silicon Valley.
```

```
I've been here since 1992, and I think I've seen
only a fraction of what California has to offer.
```

```
</End touring tip>
```

* * *

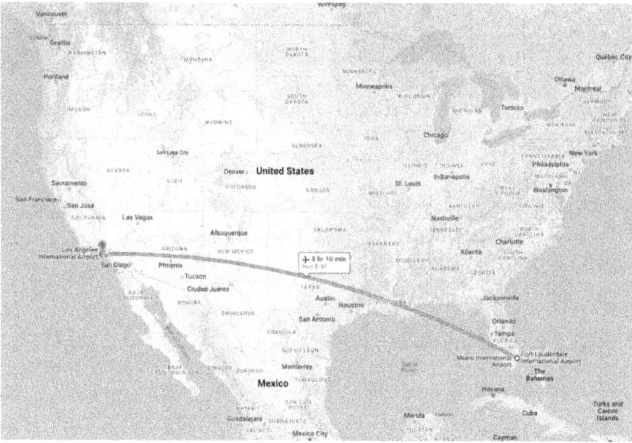

Chapter Twenty-Four

Los Angeles is a sprawling metropolitan area covering four-hundred-sixty-nine square miles of land, sandwiched between the Pacific Ocean to its west and San Bernardino National Forest to its east. It extends north through the Santa Monica Mountains and into the San Fernando Valley. It is the largest city in California and the second-largest city in the U.S., following New York City.

As our plane approached from the east, I looked out the window. The brown mountain ranges made way to the sprawling city with vertical and horizontal roads and freeways snaking through laden with heavy traffic in both directions.

```
<Begin trivia>

Los Angeles has the most complex network of
freeways in the US.

</End trivia>
```

Our plane landed at LAX. Our office was in San

Fernando Valley (aka, the Valley), which is north of the airport. We took an airport shuttle to our hotel in the city of Van Nuys (where our office was). Our driver expertly weaved through the heavy traffic, sporadically taking an exit to drive on the surface street that ran parallel to the freeway but had fewer vehicles. To appreciate his skills, you have to remind yourself that he did this in an era where there were no smartphones with Google Maps. He was solely dependent on his experience and intuitions.

```
<Begin personal observation>

Nowadays, we are so dependent on our smartphones
that they are constantly becoming smarter daily,
and we humans are becoming dumber. We tend to use
our fingertips instead of our brains.
And we call it progress.

</End personal observation>
```

Mr.R. had booked five rooms for a week and had been very generous to give us those days off to look for apartments. After driving around apartment-hunting and rejecting many, we finally liked one in Woodland Hills. It looked well maintained and new. It was a bit of a drive, but it was in the Valley.

```
<Begin tip>

If you are coming from Florida (or any other
state) with lush green vegetation, beautiful
lakes and ponds, plenty of space, and so on, you
are in for a rude surprise. The buildings are
huddled close together. The terrain is dry. It
```

becomes apparent to you as your plane is
approaching LAX. Gone are the green mountains
dotted with a body of water, replaced by brown
mountains.

The difference is even more evident now due to
the severe drought and raging wildfires.

</End tip>

When I walked into the rental office, a pleasant lady greeted us and showed us different configurations available to rent: studio, 1-bedroom, 2-bedrooms, and 3-bedrooms. I was looking to rent 2-bedrooms. There were a few to choose from, scattered across different buildings.

However, I was shocked to find out the rent was more than double for a smaller apartment. I'd be paying $1,200. I realize you will be scoffing at the amount, but it was 1992. And unlike in Florida, where ample space was available, I was assigned one spot in the underground parking (this was fine by me as I just had one vehicle.)

<Begin trivia>

Space is at a premium in Los Angeles. Many
apartment complexes only have tandem parking.

What is tandem parking? Simply put, tandem
parking means you share two parking spaces with
another person. These spaces are located one in
front of the other, which means that the person
in the back has to move their car if the person
in the front space wants to pull out.

However, having said that, L.A. is huge. As you
get farther away from the city, you will see

fewer tandem parkings. Buildings are spread out
more (and not huddled together like those you see
downtown.)

Also, you'll notice that the roads are more
expansive and street parking is unnecessary.

</End trivia>

The following day, Mr.R. sensed that I was feeling low. He asked me the reason. "What is it?" When I narrated my story to Mr. R., he just laughed. "Welcome to L.A." When he saw my sad face, he said, "L.A. is so popular that everyone wants to come here. Remember, you are getting the initial shock as you are coming from a very sparsely populated area to a highly populated one. But as time progresses, you'll get used to the pace of a big city." I soon realized that space was at a premium here; however, he was right. Since then, I've fallen in love with this place. I can't imagine myself living in any other city. L.A. is home.

Soon, and to my delight, our office moved very close to our apartment. I would come home daily for lunch. It was merely one-and-half miles away. However, I was very upset that Arun's apartment was merely a mile away :)

Sanjay and my other friend, Abhay, who had flown with us from Florida, lived in my apartment complex. And so did my other friend Keshav (who also had moved from Florida).

<Begin an Indian name pronunciation tale>
* * *

Keshav is married. His wife's name is Smriti.
It's a common name in India and can be easily
pronounced by Indians. However, our secretary at
Leadtech (who is non-Indian) had a difficult time
saying her name right. No matter how often we
tried, she would end up butchering her name.
Finally, she came to a compromise. Whenever
Smriti would call our office and ask for Keshav,
she would say, "Keshav, S-M-Riti is on the
phone." All of us Indians would burst out
laughing while our non-Indian colleagues looked
at us in confusion.

</End an Indian name pronunciation tale>

Soon, Ram C. too joined us. He had stayed behind in
Florida to finish a project. In addition to joining us,
Leadtech hired one more programmer from India,
Bharat. Yes, that Bharat. The one who was with us in
Florida. I was delighted to see him. From day one, it was
very clear in his mind. He wanted to work in the U.S. for
a few years and then return to India.

<Begin confession>

Bharat and Keshav are the only two people I know
who have returned to India after living in the
US.

</End confession>

Chapter Twenty-Five

One day, in the summer of '92, I was hacking at my keyboard in my office when my phone rang. It was the secretary. "You have a call from your attorney."

My attorney?! I was confused. "I don't have an attorney," I said aloud.

"He says he's your attorney from New Jersey."

"Ah," I exclaimed, relieved now. "He's my immigration lawyer. Put him through."

I heard a gruff voice, "Hi, it's R.B. Calling from New Jersey."

"Hello, Mr.B. (name withheld for privacy). How are you doing? Do you have some good news for me?"

"Yes, yes," he chirped. "Your application is in the cutoff date."

"*Really!*" I jumped with joy.

When DBC in New York absorbed me, I had applied for my permanent residency (a.k.a. Green Card) at Immigration and Naturalization Services (INS)—the predecessor of the Department of Homeland (DHS)[47]. Back then, INS released a 'cutoff' date every month. It was the date one applied for a Green Card. If their date fell within the cutoff date, they would be eligible for their Green Card. There was a heavy backlog. The cutoff date would move as slow as molasses. Back in Florida, I would eagerly open the Indian newspaper every month to see if I was eligible, only to be disappointed for another month. After a few months, I had tried to forget it and left it for Uncle Sam to decide my future. It seemed like a distant dream—until now. It was soon to become a reality.

"So when can you be here?" he asked.

Here? I groaned to myself as I realized what it meant. I had to go to New Jersey. Since I had applied in New York, Mr. B. had submitted all my paperwork at INS offices in New Jersey; hence, my final interview would be conducted there.

```
<Begin confession>

If I had received the call while working in
Florida, I think I would never have come to
California. It was an unknown state where I
didn't know anyone. Looking back, boy, am I glad
I came to such a beautiful state?!

</End confession>
```

"How about in two weeks?"

---

[47] On March 1, 2003, DHS absorbed the U.S. Customs Service and Immigration and Naturalization Service (INS). Source: Wikipedia.

"That works," he replied. I heard him jotting it down. "I'll make an appointment for you two weeks from today…say, 10 AM?

"Perfect," I nodded. We spoke for a little while. He walked me through the interview process. He said he would call within a few days to confirm the appointment. I thanked him and hung up. I called my wife to give her the good news and to ask her to book our airline tickets. We decided that she would go a few days early.

"Alka has been asking me for a while. I'd like to spend some time with her family." Alka was a very good friend of mine from childhood. After getting married, she came to the U.S. She and her husband, Rakesh, lived in Queens, New York.

"Okay," I agreed. "I'll join you two days before the interview."

"Why two days?"

"Just in case…," I said.

*_*_*

My flight was nonstop from LAX to LaGuardia, New York. It would depart at around one in the afternoon and reach at around nine in the evening.

```
<Begin trivia>

There's a time difference of three hours between
Los Angeles and New York. So, if my flight took
off at 1 P.M., it would be 4 P.M. there.
```

```
</End trivia>

<Begin confession>

I have to admit that I have made the mistake of
waking my friends up at midnight when it was only
9 P.M. here, not realizing that they are on the
East Coast.

</End confession>
```

My interview was a day later; hence, it would give me a day's buffer to spend time with Alka and her family. Midway through my flight, I heard the captain's voice on the speaker above me.

"Ladies and gentlemen, this is your captain speaking. I have some good news and bad news. The bad news is that LaGuardia airport is experiencing heavy rains with severe thunderstorms."

Many passengers groaned, and a murmur of dismay rose.

"However," the captain continued, "the good news is that we have over two hours of flying time. Let's all hope that it clears by the time we land. I'll keep you updated on the conditions."

The speaker went silent, and the murmur rose a decibel. Many passengers dinged the switch to call the flight attendants, who scurried through the aisles to answer them as they tried their best to sound cheerful.

My heart sank. This was not happening. *What now?* I panicked. There is absolutely no way I could afford to miss my interview. I *had* to be in New York within a day. I pressed the switch above me to call the flight attendant. A young woman walked over to me. "Yes, sir?" she pleasantly smiled as she pressed the attendant button to turn it off.

"What's happening?" I exclaimed, "do you have any additional information?"

"No, sir," she shook her head, continuing to smile. "As the captain said, we have over two hours. I'll let you know as soon as I hear anything."

"O—okay, thank you," I mumbled.

"You are welcome," she smiled, "was there anything else?"

"No," I shook my head.

"Can I get you anything? Coffee, tea, wine, beer...," she trailed off.

"A beer would be good."

"Coming right up," she chirped as she marched off to fetch me a beer.

I looked out of the window. The skies were clear, with very few clouds passing below me. I saw the shining lights on the ground, a few moving in the darkness. *Those must belong to the vehicles,* I thought. The flight attendant returned with a chilled can of beer and a packet of peanuts. I thanked her, opened the can, took a big swig, and washed it down with a handful of peanuts.

After about an hour, the captain's voice came on again. "Good evening, ladies and gentlemen." A quiet hush fell through the cabin. "I'm afraid I have some bad news.

Unfortunately, the weather conditions in LaGuardia continue to remain the same."

What does that mean? I wanted to scream. Fortunately, his following sentence gave me my answer. "That means that we won't be landing in New York. The control tower has diverted us to land in Dulles."

What? Dallas? My stomach dropped. Just then, the light attendant walked past me.

"Excuse me? Miss?" I shouted to draw her attention.

She stopped, turned around, and looked at me. "Yes?"

"Why are we going to Texas?"

"Texas?" she frowned in confusion.

"That's right. The captain just said Dallas."

"Oh," a slow smirk spread on her face as she realized my mixup. "Not Dallas, Texas but Dulles International Airport in Virginia near Washington DC."

"Oh, I see," I gave her a sheepish grin. I must have sounded like an idiot. "What happens to us then?" I said, quickly trying to cover my faux pas.

"We will arrange for your night hotel stay and fly you to New York the next morning."

My Indianness kicked in. "Do I have to pay for my stay?"

"Unfortunately, yes."

"But, why?" I protested. "It's your decision; hence, shouldn't it be your responsibility?"

"Yes, it's our decision. However, if you read the disclaimer, it clearly states—we are only responsible for a mechanical issue or a pilot shortage. This was an act of

God."

I shook my head to show my displeasure, but I realized there wasn't much I could do. I contemplated renting a car and driving to New York but quickly dismissed the insane idea.

Needless to say, I had one of the most fitful nights in the U.S. with me tossing and turning, imagining the worst-case scenarios.

*_*_*

I sighed in relief only after the wheels touched the LaGuardia landing strip and saw the familiar face of Rakesh (who had come to receive me at the airport).

Now do you, my dear readers, agree that I was not overreacting when I kept a buffer day?

Chapter Twenty-Six

In September of 1992, I went back to India for the first time since arriving in the U.S. My wife and I were super-excited. We started planning our trips months in advance. We went to the Indian strip[48] and bought the largest possible suitcases that would allow us to carry various knick-knacks. We called our families to get the shopping list. My wife then went to different stores to buy things.

```
<Begin confession>
```

```
When I look back at the things we carried on our
first trip, I smile and shake my head. Apart from
clothes, shoes, and other knick-knacks, we took
several edible items that were not readily
available in India.
```

---

[48] Little India is an Indian enclave centered on Pioneer Boulevard between 183rd and 188th streets in the city of Artesia, California. It

is the largest Indian enclave in Southern California. As of 2003, approximately 120 shops in the area catered to Indian customers. Source: Wikipedia.

* * *

</End confession>

We weighed our suitcases several times—each time adding or removing things till the needle was EXACTLY pointing to the allowed weightage and not an ounce less.

Packing for a trip back to India is an art.

*_*_*

We were flying on Singapore Airlines. Our plane would take us to Singapore, and after a very long stopover, we would take a connecting flight to Mumbai.

```
<Begin pet peeve>

After my first few trips back to India, I've
found the stopover to be long and tiring. Hence,
I prefer the Atlantic route - which flies over
the Atlantic Ocean and Europe - as opposed to the
Pacific route - which flies over the Pacific
Ocean and South Asian countries - to reach India.
In other words, I like airlines that fly over
Europe. Of course, this is a personal preference
and in no way reflects on any airline. They all
give excellent service.

</End pet peeve>
```

After landing in Singapore, the authorities there had a service where one can go and see the country for a few hours. The way it works is they keep your passport with them and put you on a bus. It then drives you around the city—making several stops at museums, promenades, and shopping areas. They then take you back to the airport, where the authorities hand you the passport (after stamping it as proof of your Singapore visit).

Even after our sightseeing excursion into the city, we still had over five hours to kill before our next flight. Singapore's massive airport has many shops, restaurants, and lounge areas. We spent the next few hours walking around and admiring various things on display.

```
<Begin confession>

The prices listed on all the items were out of my
reach. I could only look, admire and think, who
can afford to spend so much?

</End confession>
```

*_*_*

Our flying time from Singapore to Mumbai was around five hours. As the plane lowered through the clouds, I saw the land below. My heart skipped a beat.

Seeing India again after over three years.

When the tires touched the ground, and I saw the buildings zooming past first, and slowly gliding as the plane reduced its speed, I could not wipe off the silly grin on my face.

```
<Begin confession>

It's a feeling that words cannot describe.
Moreover, it's a feeling that one experiences
only once in a lifetime. It's something that can
never come back on subsequent visits. I'm sure
you, my dear reader who has returned to your
country of origin for the very first time, know
what I mean.

</End confession>
```

--*

When I came through the conveyor tunnel that connects the   plane with the airport, I ONLY saw brown faces. Moreover, I ONLY heard the familiar language of Hindi or Marathi being spoken.

I felt at home.

```
<Begin confession>

Back in the US, my ears perk-up whenever I hear
an Indian language spoken. Although I must
confess that I don't understand what is being
spoken sometimes, I know it's one the Indian
languages.

</End confession>
```

After clearing immigration and going through customs—where I had to place my bulky suitcases through an X-Ray tunnel, I placed them on the cart and made our daughter sit on top. I wheeled it toward the exit.

My parents, my brother, my wife's parents, my wife's brother and many of my friends had come to receive us. They all were smiling while waving frantically. My smile widened when I saw them. I quickened the wheeling of the cart. They were standing behind the steel barrier that separated the arriving passenger. They all were looking at our daughter in person for the very first time. When I neared them, I lifted our daughter to hold her in my arms and handed her to my mother. I touched my parents feet and hugged my brother. I then hugged my friends. However, our daughter was the center-of-attention. She was being handed over from one relative to another while being pinched in her cheeks by my friends.

```
<Begin confession>
```

```
She looked confused and harassed. She might have
thought, who are all these strangers who know my
name?
```

```
</End confession>
```

On the very first morning in India, my father had arranged for the local barber to come home and give me a shave. He would come home for the next thirty days to give home service. All I had to do was to sit in a chair and lift my chin. He would lather my face, shave once with a fresh blade, lather it again, shave it one more time. He then would cover my face with a warm towel. In the end, he would pat it with some after-shave. Once every three days, he also would act as a male masseuse. He would first massage my head with coconut oil and then my entire body. By the time he was done, I would doze off.

```
<Begin confession>
```

```
I was thoroughly pampered for the next thirty
days and I enjoyed every minute of it.
```

```
</End confession>
```

* * *

After spending thirty days with my friends and family, going to my favorite restaurants, going to the nearby hill station, *Matheran* for a few days, having endless debates with my father (he loved to debate), meeting my *mamas* & *mamis* (maternal uncles and aunts) *kaka* & *kaki* (paternal uncle and aunt) etc., it was time to go back.

```
<Begin clarification>

Previously I mentioned that the maternal aunt is
called masi. Not mami. That's correct. A mother's
sister is called masi and her husband is called
masa. Whereas a mother's brother is called mama
and his wife mami. And to make things more
confusing, these words are specific ONLY to some
languages. They are called something totally
different in another language.

</End clarification>
```

The mood at the airport was a mixture of sadness and joy. My wife was to stay behind with our daughter for one more month.

As the plane took off, I could not help but reflect back on the past thirty days.

Chapter Twenty-Seven

My friend and colleague, Abhay, had come to receive me. As I exited the arrival area, I saw him standing behind the steel barriers. He waved at me. I waved back and navigated my cart to him. I shook his hand. "Hi."

"Welcome back," he smiled.

I could not help noticing the stark difference between my two arrivals. When I arrived in India, I saw the joy on many familiar faces. There was happiness all around me. It was an exhilarating feeling that lasted for thirty days (well, if not for thirty days, a very long time.)

We walked to the parking structure and loaded my suitcases in his car. We drove north on the 405 to the Valley.

"So, how was your trip?" Abhay asked me cheerfully.

"Wonderful," I replied in a monosyllable, still missing my family.

"That's great. You look relaxed, man."

"Yeah, thanks," I answered as I continued looking out the window. He must have realized that I wanted to be left alone, so he fell quiet. We drove in silence for the rest of the journey.

Soon, we made our way up the 405 and headed west on 101 after crossing the Santa Monica Mountains. I looked at Abhay. He was concentrating on the road, but he had a severe expression. I looked ahead. We were around ten minutes from our exit.

He looked straight ahead at the traffic. "There's something I have to tell you."

"What is it?" I asked him. I was alarmed now. He glanced at me momentarily. *Do I detect sadness on his face? Or is it pity?*

"Abhay, what is it?!" I raised my voice. Alarm bells were going off now.

"Your apartment was burglarized," he said softly.

"*Huh?*" I went numb. I thought I had misheard him. I wanted to *mishear* him. "W—what?" I stammered. "You are joking, right?"

He finally looked at me. I saw the pain in his eyes. I immediately knew he wasn't. "No," he shook his head. A chill ran up my spine.

"H—how? W—what? W—when? W—hat?" I stammered, unaware of what I was saying. Beads of sweat formed on my forehead. I couldn't breathe. I rolled down the window.

Mixed emotions were running through my mind. Fear and anger were at the top, followed by a feeling of violation and vulnerability.

"When did this happen?"

"Last night...I think," I had asked him to keep an eye on our apartment. He would check it daily to make sure that it was secured. I had also given him the keys so he could go in and check on things. I had also registered him as my emergency contact with the rental office.

"*You think!?*" I looked at him in disbelief. "Why do you *think* that might have happened?" I said sarcastically.

```
<Begin confession>

Looking back, I think I was a little harsh on
him. However, in my defense, I had just arrived
from India and felt low, all alone, etc. I now
can look back and narrate my ordeal. But, it took
me a long time to get over it.

</End confession>
```

"I would check your apartment daily. I would also go into it every other day to ensure everything was okay. I checked your apartment's door last evening. It was well-secured."

"Oh," I said. I had completely forgotten about our arrangement. "Sorry," I apologized.

"No need for that," he smiled. "I'll ask you to do the same when I go to India."

"Of course," I nodded. "Then how did you find out?"

"I got a call from the rental office this morning."

"Oh," I nodded. It made sense now. However, the fear, the vulnerability, and the feeling of being violated still hung like a dark cloud. I looked at him. "What happens now?"

"The rental office has already notified the authorities about the incident. A police officer should come here tomorrow to write a report."

"Was anything taken?"

"I don't know," he shook his head, "I didn't check on your apartment today. I came directly from work to get you."

"Oh," I mumbled.

We exited and drove past the chained gates that guarded the apartment complex. They were kept wide-open during the day. *What a false sense of security,* I thought.

As the elevator stopped on the first floor and I wheeled my suitcase to the apartment, my jaw dropped. The wood had been chipped where the lock was. The door was slightly ajar. Abhay was right behind me. Gingerly, I pushed it open, bracing myself to see the worst. However (and to my relief), everything looked in place. I quickly checked the bedrooms. Nothing seemed to be missing.

I then noticed a drawer next to the bathroom. It was open. That's where my wife would keep her ornaments. (thankfully, we didn't have much). Abhay, too, noticed the open drawer.

"Oh, no!" he exclaimed. I was busy rummaging through it, unsure of what I was looking for.

"Anything missing?" he asked.

"I don't know," I shook my head as I continued to open jewelry boxes. "My wife usually knows what is in here."

However, I knew that we had recently opened a safe

deposit box. But I didn't know if she had put our valuables there.

I desperately hoped she had.

*_*_*

Needless to say, I had the most horrendous night. I couldn't sleep. I was unable to lock the door, having terrifying thoughts of their return—only to find out the apartment was occupied this time and the burglar was shooting at me in a panic.

After all, this is a country that loves guns.

Only when morning sunlight seeped through the vertical blinds could I feel a little courage returning to me.

I called my wife in India and informed her that I was safely back in the US. I was also relieved that she had gone to the bank to keep our valuables in the safe deposit box.

```
<Begin confession>

She, however, must have been wondering about my
sudden interest in our jewelry. I decided to
break the news after a few days when things had
cooled down a little, and I knew more.

</End confession>
```

*_*_*

The following day, the building maintenance man came by and fixed the lock. It gave me a little mental relief, but I was still frazzled by the previous day's emotional turmoil and the lack of sleep. The two-inch thick wooden door seemed more like a mental comfort than a physical barrier.

Later that afternoon, I heard a knock on my door. I opened it, hoping to see the sympathetic face of Abhay or Sanjay, but instead, I was greeted by a burly police officer. He wore a blue uniform. He held a plastic forensic kit in his left hand.

"Hello, I'm Officer Robinson from L.A.P.D.," he nodded slightly. "Did you report a burglary?"

"Yes, yes," I smiled and nodded, swinging open the door wider, "come in, Officer Robinson." He entered the room and looked around.

"This way, please," I gestured towards my bedroom and started walking. He followed me.

I took him to the drawer and opened it. "Here."

"Thanks," he nodded as he placed the forensic kit on the top of the drawer and butterflied it open. He reached for a pair of blue gloves and wiggled his burly fingers until they snugly fit. Next, he took out a soft brush and a bottle containing black powder. He twisted open the cap and dabbed the brush in it. When he was satisfied that it had collected enough particles, he swiped the surface of the drawer. He let it settle for a moment and extracted a transparent plastic tape. He cut a portion from it and stuck it on the residues made by the brush. He then dabbed it a few times, ripped it from the surface, and held it against the overhead light.

"Damn," he groaned.

I was watching the whole routine with utter fascination.

"What?" I asked.

"Didn't pick up any."

"Pickup what?"

"Fingerprints," he looked at me nonchalantly.

"Oh, wow," I looked at him, wide-eyed. "What if you had picked up any?"

"I would have run them against our database of known criminals," he shrugged.

"Wow," I was impressed but wanted to know more. "Tell me, Officer, do you ever catch criminals this way?"

"Honestly," he confided in me, "the success rates are not very good in such cases. After all, we consider them as those with the lowest priority."

"What do you mean 'the lowest priority?'" I asked him indignantly. Wasn't my case important? After all, a crime had been committed. I expected the full force of the L.A.P.D. to divert its full resources to solve it. Thanks to watching too many Hollywood movies, I wanted a dozen cop cars with their trademark white-and-blue lights turned on to come rushing to the crime scene with their sirens blazing. And within twenty-four hours, they would apprehend the burglar.

"This is categorized as a petty theft and not a murder case," his words brought me down to earth. "We divert very few resources, if any, to such cases. Thus, usually, they go unsolved."

"Oh, I see." I was disappointed.

"Besides," he continued, "no physical harm was done to anyone, right?"

"Right." I nodded.

"Well then, there is nothing more for me to do here," he waved dismissively as he closed his kit. He took out a form and started to write on it. When he was done, he tore a copy and handed it to me. "This is for you."

"Thank you," I took it, folded it, and pocketed it. He walked to the door, turned around, and shook my hand. "We'll call you if we know something."

"Thank you, Officer," I nodded, but we both knew the matter had ended there. He probably would go back and file a report that would be added to one of the thousands of unsolved cases.

It was an earth-shattering experience for me but a very routine one for him.

Chapter Twenty-Eight

The burglary had left me feeling vulnerable. On top of that, I was feeling lonely in a two-bedroom apartment. Even in my office, my work began to suffer. Everyone could tell I was lacking my usual cheerful self. As any programmer can testify, it requires concentration for long periods. It's not a mechanical job. My boss, Mr.R., would find me staring out of the window. He was kind enough to give me a few days off.

Abhay, who was good friends with Anjali, told her about my state. She was staying in a cute little house with white picket fences in Long Beach with her husband, Shreekant. She called me.

"What's up?"

"Not much," I mumbled, not in the mood for a long conversation.

"How was India?"

"Good."

```
<Begin confession>
```

* * *

Looking back, I must have sounded like a jerk.
Usually, I am a good conversationalist.

</End confession>

"When are they coming back?"

I knew who 'they' were. "In a month."

"Oh,"

"Yeah," I sighed.

"Okay, here's what I want you to do. And I won't take no for an answer," she said with resolve.

"What?"

"I want you to come and spend the weekend with us."

"B—but," I began to protest.

"No buts," she cut me off. "We'll see you on Friday."

Before I could come up with any further excuses, she hung up the phone.

*_*_*

On Friday, I drove south on 405 to Long Beach. Even though they live far away from the Valley, it was worth it. I felt at home with their company and delicious Indian meals freshly prepared by Anjali. When she was cooking, the familiar aroma of a mixture of spices wafting through the kitchen tingled my senses. It took me back to India. Indian food is not just aromatic to smell and taste but also whisks one to their days in India.

After spending the weekend with them, my mood uplifted. I was ready to go back to work.

When it was time for me to return, Anjali packed Indian food for me to carry back to my apartment. This may sound trivial to many, but Indian food is vital to us Indians (especially bachelors).

The ubiquity of Indian restaurants and grocery stores has been a significant relief; however, back then, they were scarce.

I spent the next few weeks looking forward to my wife's return. I would dread the evenings—the time after I got off from work and the time I went to sleep. The very thought of going back to an empty apartment would give me chills. I would work a few more hours (until the last person left for the day). I didn't want to be the only person at work. I still was fearful of being alone. When I would be in my apartment, I would jump at the slightest noise. I would turn on the TV and increase its volume or play the music loudly until my neighbor banged on my door to complain of the loud noise.

```
<Begin confession>
```

```
You, my dear reader, may find it amusing, but in
my defense, this was the first time in my twenty-
eight-year on this earth that I was ever alone.
```

```
</End confession>
```

However, fortunately, my friends once again came to my rescue. I would spend time playing racquetball with Abhay and my new friend, Shiva, or would go golfing with Shiva, Abhay, and Sanjay.

```
<Begin confession>
```

* * *

Shiva introduced me to the beautiful game of golf (which can start as a relaxing stroll in a lush garden and end up being frustrating and hair-pulling). Also, like me, Shiva is a lefty (he plays left-handed). He already had invested in various golf clubs. Hence, I was glad to 'borrow' his set.

Moreover, Shiva, Sanjay, and I are huge cricket fans who hail from the same city, Mumbai. Thus, we had too many common interests. In addition to that, since we come from the same city, our dialect of Hindi is the same. Whereas Ram C. And Arun come from a different state where they speak differently. It's not that different that we can't understand each other, but we know they are not talking 'Bambaiya' Hindi (which, I must confess, can sound atrocious to those who speak a purer form of Hindi.)
Pankaj, my friend from New Delhi, always found our Hindi laughable. People there speak a purer form of Hindi.

However, having said that, I feel that the essential factor is that we communicate with each other in a language we are all comfortable in. Yes, we often find ourselves making fun of each other about how they speak or the word they use, but we all know that it's in jest.

It's always healthier to find common ground than to think of things that can drive us apart.

<End confession>

We would either go out to one of our favorite restaurants to have dinner, or go to one of their houses (all were bachelors then) and spend the evening listening to

Bollywood songs from yesteryears while cooking. Fortunately, unlike me, they all had excellent culinary skills. It was self-evident that they knew their way around the kitchen and what they were doing. I would gladly volunteer to be the sous-chef, making myself useful in the kitchen by washing and chopping vegetables. Ram C. (who had joined us from Florida) would also be part of our 'festivities.'

```
<Begin disclaimer>

Allow me to set the record straight. I'm not
claiming that they were a 'Michelin-star-chef.'
However, as far as I was concerned, they were. In
addition to that, they were all engineers. Hence,
they tended to treat cooking more like a science
than an art.

</End disclaimer>
```

Even now, we sometimes fondly reminisce about our 'good old days.'

At the risk of sounding preachy, the lesson I've learned from one of my most traumatic experiences is—this too shall pass. However, I must say that when you are going through the experience, if someone tells you that, you may feel like punching them.

Chapter Twenty-Nine

On January 17th, 1994, at around 4:30 AM, we were hit by a massive earthquake (6.7 on the Richter scale). It caused severe damage to many structures. It lasted approximately 10-20 seconds but was long enough to create havoc. The shaking was felt as far as San Diego, Las Vegas, Phoenix, etc.—hundreds of miles from its epicenter in Northridge, which is around thirty miles away from our apartment. Two 6.0 Mw aftershocks followed, the first one about one minute after the initial event and the second approximately 11 hours later, the strongest of several thousand aftershocks. The death toll was 57, with more than 9,000 injured. In addition, property damage was estimated to be $13–50 billion (equivalent to $24–93 billion in 2021), making it one of the costliest natural disasters in U.S. history.

I was asleep in the bedroom of our apartment. My wife was sleeping beside me, and our four-year-old daughter was sandwiched between us. Although she had her own room, she preferred to sleep in-between us.

Suddenly, the entire apartment began to sway and shake. Having lived through several mild ones (California is an earthquake country), I had experienced the feeling of gentle rolling that usually lasted for five seconds. Most of the time, the epicenter was hundreds of miles away: in the mountains, in the desert, or a city with a far smaller population. Thus, the damage was less severe (hardly any if it was in the mountains or the desert). In addition, California has a strict building code. The builder has to comply with it while laying down the foundation.

* * *

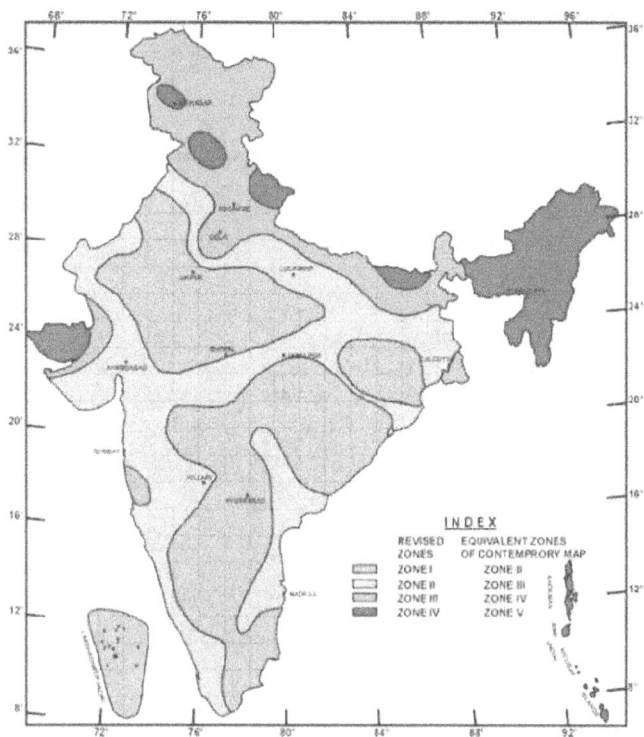

By the way, Mumbai is in Zone 3 as per the
Seismic Atlas of India, which has a moderate
risk, but that is not all. The tall skyscrapers
in the city are not built to any earthquake code.
There is no earthquake code for tall towers.

</End comparison>

However, this was nothing like the mild ones I had
experienced in the past. I had experienced earthquakes
that lasted between five to ten seconds. However, this one
was louder, more violent, and lasted longer. Although it
lasted between ten and twenty seconds, those ten to

twenty seconds seemed like an eternity. I felt it would never end.

I can keep describing how horrific the experience was, but unless you endure the same, words are not enough to describe it (and I pray that no one should go through it.)

```
<Begin the difference>

The cluster of states in the midwestern U.S.
where tornadoes are most likely to occur is known
as tornado alley. Tornado alley typically
includes parts of Texas, Oklahoma, Kansas,
Nebraska, South Dakota, Indiana, Missouri, Iowa,
Illinois, and Ohio.

Then ten eastern states of the U.S. are
identified as hurricane states. They are Florida,
North Carolina, Louisiana, South Carolina,
Alabama, Georgia, Mississippi, New York,
Virginia, and Texas.

However, there is a significant difference
between these two disasters and an earthquake.

Unlike these states, where people get a warning
in advance that a tornado or a hurricane is
headed their way, so they have time to prepare,
there is no warning in an earthquake. In one
second, your life can turn upside-down.

</End the difference>
```

Once again, I digress.

Instinctively, I rolled over to cover our daughter and my wife.

"What's happening?" she screamed.

"It's an earthquake," I yelled back.

* * *

```
<Begin confession>

I have never felt so helpless in my life before.
There was nothing I could do but wait for the
tremors to get over.

</End confession>
```

I thought it would never end. This was it. We all were going to die. But mercifully, the shaking stopped as suddenly as it had started. We were engulfed in darkness and silence. I heard the walls creaking as the structure tried to settle down in its base. I reached under the lampshade next to my bed and tried to turn it on, but to no avail. There was no power. I opened the drawer of the side table next to my bed, rummaged through it until my hands felt the circular shape of the flashlight, and flicked it on. The ghostly shadows cast on the walls. I aimed the beam down to the carpet and walked out.

"Be careful," my wife shouted. "Things must have fallen."

Gingerly, I stepped out into my living room. I swung the beam around to survey the damage quickly. Nothing. Everything appeared in its place. I walked across to the kitchen.

My jaw dropped.

The kitchen cabinets had flung open, and dishes, glasses, vases, and many other things were lying on the floor. Each and every glassware was shattered into thousands of tiny pieces. I opened my shoe closet, wore my shoes, and took a pair for my wife and daughter. I ran back to the bedroom and asked my wife to change into pants and a tee-shirt (she was in her nightdress) and put shoes on our daughter's feet. We quickly exited the apartment building and stood out in the open. All the other residents also had done the same. Some of them were still in pajamas and fluffy sandals, while some ladies had wrapped a comforter to cover their lacy negligees.

They all looked stunned.

Soon, we could hear sirens all around us. I could not tell the difference between an alarm blaring from the building or the sirens wailing from the emergency vehicles. The earthquake was so massive and widespread that there were not enough emergency personnel to attend to the needs of thousands.

Chapter Thirty

Soon, Federal Emergency Management Agency (FEMA) came to our aid. Many structures were damaged. The building inspectors were going from one building to another to certify if they were safe for humans. They would do an initial 'quick survey' to determine the structure's safety. They then would tag it green, orange, or red. Green meant it was safe to go in and red indicated that one was not allowed to go in. Residents of these buildings could not even enter the building for a few minutes to gather their belongings. They would have to find an alternative place to stay and go there literally with the shirts on their backs (a favorite thing for FOBs to say as in, "son, when I came to this country, I had nothing but a shirt on my back.") Orange was the diciest one of them. It meant "go at your own risk," and to make matters more unpredictable, it also meant that the inspectors might red-tag it later. We had a tiny window in-between them returning for a detailed inspection and red-tagging our building. If that happened, we would not be allowed in. We would have to find a safe place to stay with literally nothing but the shirts on our backs. I didn't have anything else on my person: no wallet—which meant no driving license or social security card (to prove my identity). I would be back to square one. I would have to reset my life with a fresh start.

Needless to say, I was torn between going in to take my stuff or finding a safe place to stay. I spoke with Keshav (who lived in the same building). We then called Shiva (who is a civil engineer). He resided in Burbank, away from the Valley. Although he had felt the earthquake, his house was farther away from the epicenter, thus, less vulnerable to the earthquake. Still, we wanted to ensure that it was habitable. I also wasn't too sure if others from the Valley had called him already and if he had committed to them staying. He had many friends in the Valley. I feared that someone else had already called him.

I dialed his number. After a few rings, he answered. "Are you ok?"

"Yes," he replied, "are you?"

"Well…," I started, "yes and no."

"What do you mean?"

"Yes, we all are physically fine. However, we are now homeless."

"Huh? Did you say homeless?"

"Yes," I nodded.

"What do you mean 'homeless?'"

I explained to him my situation. He listened to it attentively. "I see," he finally said. I held my breath as I waited for his answer. I wasn't sure if he already had committed to someone. Apart from him, I knew no one else in the Valley. The only other person I knew in L.A. was Anjali. However, she stayed in Long Beach—which was miles away from us. Even if I had moved to her house, it would be a nightmare to commute to work daily. It would take me around two hours of driving (each way) in the rush hour traffic.

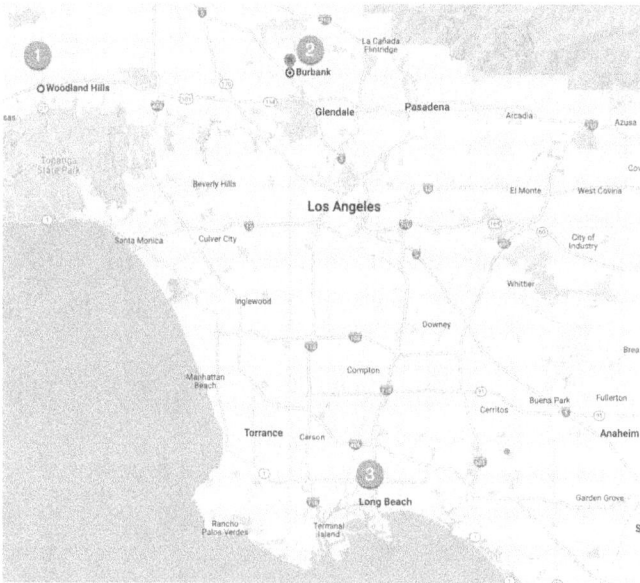

1=My Apartment 2=Shiva's house 3=Anjali's house

<Begin freeway driving tales>

Although L.A. has the most comprehensive network of freeways in the US, it is called the parking lot. There are way too many vehicles on the road. For every Los Angelino, it's normal to proudly talk about how they shaved off a few minutes of drive time by taking a particular route. For an outsider, it may seem a bit bizarre, but for us, it's a valuable piece of information.

In fact, on the T.V. show Saturday Night Live there is a skit called The Californians where they talk about nothing but the route they took to reach their destination.

</End freeway driving tales>

Yes, Sanjay and Ram C. too lived in Burbank, but they lived in a 1-bedroom apartment. It wasn't equipped for us (neither was Shiva's, but he had a house). Besides, they lived in an apartment complex, which meant they would have to follow the rules in the lease agreement. So, even if they wanted to accommodate us, they couldn't. Otherwise, they would be running the risk of being evicted. I would be responsible for making them homeless too.

Shiva was my only hope. *Please let him say yes,* I prayed. *Please let him not have committed to anyone else.*

He made it easy for me to decide with four words.

"Come stay with me."

Yes, I pumped my fist. I felt as if an enormous burden had been lifted off of my shoulders. We had a place to stay.

I sprang into action. I rented a U-Haul truck, loaded it with whatever little I could take with me, and drove to Shiva's house. I didn't take a single piece of furniture or crockery with me.

It's a single-family, two-storied house on a quiet and sleepy street heavily shaded with tall trees, the emphasis being on single-family, which is meant for a family of four. However, we were nine. Three in my family + Keshav and Smriti + Bharat, Manasi, and their 7-month-old son, Abhishek + Shiva.

We all spent the next few days in a daze. Shiva was kind enough to give up his bed to let the three of us sleep on it while he slept on the carpeted floor. We all were jittery. The slightest sound that was out of the ordinary would make us jump. I rented an apartment in Burbank in a hurry. I was afraid of it not staying on the market for long as many families like me were suddenly homeless. Keshav, too, found an apartment in Burbank. Ram C. and Sanjay were already renting an apartment in Burbank; hence, it was a no-brainer for us. Arun had moved south to Orange County; therefore, he was not impacted as severely as we did.

It was the most stressful period in our lives, and Shiva came to our rescue. I genuinely believe in the saying, घर नहीं, दिल बड़ा चाहिए (not the house but the heart should be big).

2023

Chapter Thirty-One

As I look back on my life, if someone asked me to sum it up in a word, it would be: thankful. Thankful to Donn for selecting me. Thankful to the lady at the US Consulate who changed my life by granting me a visa. Thankful to Aruna *masi*, Chandrakant *masa*, Paresh, and Anjali for starting my new life in a foreign country. Thankful to Chakshu *kaki* and Niranjan *kaka* for taking us home when our daughter was born on a snowy January. Thankful to my family and friends for being with me on my colorful journey. Thankful to innumerable people who enriched my life.

Yes, my journey may be colorful but not unique. I'm sure every immigrant has a story to tell. For example, Shiva had to spend five days at the JFK International Airport—when he first came to this country—before he flew to South Dakota to his university. Or he had to go for groceries in a car without any backseats; hence, he had to carry his own chair when he had to go grocery shopping during the bitter South Dakota winter.

Or Kevin getting shot. Or Ram C. getting mugged on his last day in New York—before he flew to Florida.

When I came to this country, I was the apex stone of a pyramid, supported by others. As time has progressed, I've moved down the pyramid to become a supporting stone for a newcomer to be the apex. Will you be a support stone to help someone on the pinnacle?

When I see the young generation expanding their wings in fields other than medicine and engineering, I'm engulfed with satisfying warmth.

```
<Begin disclaimer>

There is absolutely nothing wrong with being an
engineer. There are many success stories of such
talents rising to the top. A few that come to
mind are Google's CEO, Sunder Pichai, Microsoft's
CEO, Satya Nadella, Adobe's CEO Shantanu Narayen,
IBM's CEO, Arvind Krishna, and Twitter's Ex-CEO,
Parag Agrawal.

In addition to being Indians, we have one more
thing in common. We all are FOBs. (and are
cricket fans).

</End disclaimer>
```

Recently, India celebrated seventy-five years of independence. The transformation from a developing country to a thriving economy boasting the youngest labor force in the world is drastic. I'm merely a cog in the wheel of a flourishing country. When I see the twinkle in the eyes of the young generation in India, I see a dream of making their own country successful instead of migrating to another nation.

Having said that, the US is still a land of opportunities. Albeit, it's getting harder, it's not impossible. When I came to this country, I thought that I was a late arrival. But now, when I look back at the advances science and technology have made, I feel that I was one of the fortunate ones to arrive early.

If a mere B.Sc. graduate from the vernacular medium can make it, so can you.

I still remember the tagline for the New York Lottery: All you need is a dollar and a dream. It still is applicable to those who dream of success in the land of opportunity.

All you need are a few dollars and a dream.

Here I Am :

Far away now I am from my homeland
with treasure of memories of my prime.
Grateful I am to the land where I stand,
yet heart goes back and forth from time to time.
My road of gentle pace and aimless drifts
tarred with turmoils and peace, darkness and light.
Of twists and turns spiced with numerous shifts.
From financial plight to some soulful sights.
Sometimes I wonder what would I have been
had I not trodden this once unknown road?
But play of fate is forever unseen.
All you need is a wheel of will to goad.
Often unaware these are pleasure-walks.
And though loud it ticktocks, blind is the clock.

Acknowledgment

As you can tell by the quality of my writing, I'm not a writer, nor do I consider myself to be one. For example, I'm always confused about the placement of a period or comma in parentheses—*does it go BEFORE or AFTER the parentheses*. So, I googled. And my confusion was crystal clear when I got 'it depends.' I can already see the grammar police cracking their knuckles to fire off an email, pointing out the holes in my writing.

In my defense, I merely wanted to narrate my experiences in an easy-to-read language where one doesn't get distracted by unknown words. Unlike many talented writers, I don't find myself compelled to write. I pen down my thoughts when I get an idea of an exciting story.

My wife asked me a simple question when I wrote my first book. "Point me to a book that is similar to your story." And honestly, I couldn't think of a single title, nor could I answer her next question. "What's your target audience?" If you look at the books I've written so far, you'll see that I'm all over the genre map.

However, there's one thing in common. I've had help, support, and input from my friends and family. When I read other books, the author thanks agents, publishers, designers, editors, etc. I've always wondered how many of those are the author's actual friends. On the other hand, I can say that I personally know each and every person who has helped me in various stages of creating this book.

I'd like to thank my sister-in-law for her invaluable input in suggesting the addition to the title and editing the book, my brother for composing the beautiful poem, and my friends Inbar, Shiva, and Bharat for suggesting edits.

Inbar has been the first editor of my book, he is EXACTLY what I'd expect. I believe that there are many line editors and copy editors. However, he has also been my technical editor (being in the computer-field) and also, being a non-Indian, has asked me for many clarifications for trivial matters that me being an Indian has taken for granted. In addition to that, he has been my 'political police.'

Thank you, Pankaj, Keshav, Ram C., Arun, Sanjay, and Abhay, for your invaluable input. Thank you, my 'partners-in-crime,' Rahul and Rajul—who came to this country with me. I'd like to thank Donn Liles for his invaluable input. I'd like to thank Ashok Arora for a memorable experience.

I wouldn't have had it easy were it not for Aruna *masi*, Chandrakant *masa*, Paresh, and Anjali. Or my wife's uncle and aunt, Niranjan *kaka* and Chakshu *kaki*. Or my wife's friend and her husband, Anjali, and Shreekant. Or my friend and her husband, Alka, and Rakesh.

Although I've not met Mr. Narayana Murthy in person, I'd like to thank him for my very first introduction to CAMP.

Writing this book has been a pleasure…a stroll down memory lane. What a journey has it been?!

Other Books

The Galaxy Series

#1. Beyond The Milky Way

#2. Return To Earth

#3. Divided States of America

#4. 2120

Website: thegalaxyseries.com
Facebook: facebook.com/thegalaxyseriesbooks

India Was One

Website: indiawasone.com
Facebook: facebook.com/indiawasone

The Man From Afghanistan